D1598086

The Incomplete Universe

The Incomplete Universe
Totality, Knowledge, and Truth

Patrick Grim

A Bradford Book
The MIT Press
Cambridge, Massachusetts
London, England

© 1991 Massachusetts Institute of Technology

All rights reserved. No part of this book may be reproduced in any form by any electronic or mechanical means (including photocopying, recording, or information storage and retrieval) without permission in writing from the publisher.

BD
171
.G765
1991

This book was set in Times Roman by Asco Trade Typesetting Ltd., Hong Kong, and was printed and bound in the United States of America.

Library of Congress Cataloging-in-Publication Data

Grim, Patrick.
  The incomplete universe: totality, knowledge, and truth / Patrick Grim.
      p.   cm.
  "A Bradford book."
  Includes bibliographical references and index.
  ISBN 0-262-07134-7
  1. Truth. 2. Certainty. I. Title.
  BD171.G765   1991
  121—dc20   91-13555
                                                                  CIP

To the memory of my father, Elgas Grim

Contents

Preface

Over the past seven years major pieces of the argument have been developed and refined in article form. Though perhaps here transformed and restructured beyond recognition, some portions of the work that follows have appeared in "Some Neglected Problems of Omniscience," *American Philosophical Quarterly*; "There Is No Set of All Truths," *Analysis*; "On Sets and Worlds: A Reply to Menzel," *Analysis*; "Truth, Omniscience, and the Knower," *Philosophical Studies*; "Logic and Limits of Knowledge and Truth," *Noûs*; "On Situations and the World: A Problem for Barwise and Etchemendy" (with Gary Mar), *Analysis*; and "On Omniscience and a 'Set of All Truths': A Reply to Bringsjord," *Analysis*. Though my work on essential indexicals has been instrumental in the development of this set of ideas, it forms a conceptually distinct topic in many ways, and for that reason I have not included it here. The interested reader is referred in particular to "Against Omniscience: The Case from Essential Indexicals," in *Noûs*.

I have many people to thank. I am deeply indebted to Geoffrey Hunter, Michael Slote, and Hector-Neri Castañeda for encouragement at crucial junctures. For help in discussion and correspondence on various topics at various points, I am grateful to C. Anthony Anderson, David Auerbach, Kit Fine, Allen Hazen, Douglas Hofstadter, Christopher J. Martin, Elliot Mendelson, Christopher Menzel, Alvin Plantinga, John Post, Rudy Rucker, Wilfrid Sieg, Jordan Howard Sobel, Kriste Taylor, Neil Tennant, Edward Wierenga, and Hao Wang. A special debt in this regard is owed to David Boyer, Robert F. Barnes, Evan W. Conyers, and Gary Mar. A still deeper debt, of a different sort, I owe to those close to me for their loving support throughout the project.

The Incomplete Universe

God created all in number, weight and measure. He enumerates the number of the stars, of the grains of sand on the seashore, of the scales of the fishes. He knows how many truths there are and how many [propositions] are true. This we will easily enough allow; whether it be two or a hundred or a thousand that are true, He knows it. But He does not know some collection of truths beyond which there are no more [truths]. For there are none such.
Ars Meliduna, *ca. 1150*

To sum up: it appears that the special contradiction of Chapter x is solved by the doctrine of types, but that there is at least one closely analogous contradiction which is probably not soluble by this doctrine. The totality of all logical objects, or of all propositions, involves, it would seem, a fundamental logical difficulty. What the complete solution of the difficulty may be, I have not succeeded in discovering; but as it affects the very foundations of reasoning, I earnestly commend the study of it to the attention of all students of logic.
The closing lines of Russell's Principles of Mathematics, *1903*

Introduction: Some Philosophical Fragments

This is an exploration of a cluster of related logical results. Taken together, these seem to have something philosophically important to teach us: something about knowledge and truth and something about the logical impossibility of *totalities* of knowledge and truth.

The chapters that follow include explorations of new forms of the ancient and venerable paradox of the Liar, applications and extensions of Kaplan and Montague's paradox of the Knower, generalizations of Gödel's work on incompleteness, and new uses of Cantorian diagonalization. Throughout, however, my concern is with metaphysical and epistemological *implications* of these results: what such results may have to teach us about knowledge and truth. In particular, I think, these may have something to teach us about the incoherence of a notion of *all* truth or of *total* knowledge.

Let me try to sketch more clearly the general vision of the work that follows by beginning with three philosophical fragments. Each of these is, of course, important in its own right. I evoke them here, however, for the sake of illustration. For what the results of following chapters seem to suggest is that each of these fragments is fatally flawed.

The first fragment is this: the notion of possible worlds, though, of course, tracing back to Leibniz, has been of major importance for the semantics of modal logic and for contemporary metaphysics over the last twenty years. But what are possible worlds supposed to be? One approach is to treat possible worlds as maximal consistent sets of propositions—proposition-saturated sets to which no further proposition can be added without precipitating inconsistency—or as some sort of fleshed-out correlates to such sets.[1] The *actual* world, on such an account, is that maximal and consistent set of propositions all members of which actually obtain—a maximal and consistent set of all truths—or is an appropriately fleshed-out correlate to such a set.

The second fragment is this: Gaunilo, a contemporary of Anselm's, parodied Anselm's ontological argument for the existence of God by constructing a parallel argument for the existence of the lost island, "more excellent than all other lands." Alvin Plantinga, in defending a contemporary modal form of Anselm's argument for a greatest possible being, attempts to avoid a corresponding modal form of Gaunilo's argument for a greatest possible island. He does so by insisting that the great-making characteristics of islands, unlike those of an Anselmian God, are without *intrinsic maxima*:

The idea of an island than which it's not possible that there be a greater is like the idea of a natural number than which it's not possible that there be a greater.... There neither is nor could be a greatest possible natural number; indeed, there isn't a greatest *actual* number, let alone a greatest possible. And the same goes for islands. No matter how great an island is, no matter how many Nubian maidens and dancing girls adorn it, there could always be a greater—one with twice as many, for example. The qualities that make for greatness in islands—numbers of palm trees, amount and quality of coconuts, for example—most of these qualities have no *intrinsic maximum*. That is, there is no degree of productivity or number of palm trees (or of dancing girls) such that it is impossible that an island display more of that quality. So the idea of a greatest possible island is an inconsistent or incoherent idea; it's not possible that there be such a thing....

But doesn't Anselm's argument founder on the same rock? If the idea of a greatest possible island is inconsistent, won't the same hold for the idea of a greatest possible being? Perhaps not.... Anselm clearly has in mind such properties as wisdom, knowledge, power, and moral excellence or moral perfection. And certainly knowledge, for example, does have an *intrinsic maximum*. (Plantinga 1974a, 90–91)[2]

Consider as a third philosophical fragment the opening lines of the *Tractatus*:

1* The world is all that is the case.

1.1 The world is the totality of facts, not of things.

1.11 The world is determined by the facts, and by their being *all* the facts. (Wittgenstein 1921)

What the following chapters suggest is that each of these three fragments harbors a deep and pervasive error—a fundamental mistake regarding the nature of knowledge or truth.

By a Cantorian argument which appears most explicitly in chapter four, for example, closely related to arguments in chapters three and one, it appears that any set of true propositions will prove incomplete: that any set of true propositions will leave some true proposition out. If so, of course, there can be no maximal set of truths. If possible worlds are to be outlined as in the first fragment above, it appears, there can be no *actual* world.

The work of chapter four indicates, moreover, that Cantorian difficulties of the sort at issue are by no means limited to standard sets, that they will apply against a proper or ultimate class of all truths as well, for example, and will hold even within a theory deprived of the power set axiom. In the end, such arguments raise serious questions regarding propositional quantification as well.

In the second fragment Plantinga's defense of the Anselmian argument crucially depends on there being an intrinsic maximum for powers that appear among the divine attributes. "And certainly knowledge, for example, does have an *intrinsic maximum.*"

What the results of following chapters seem to indicate, however, is that knowledge does *not* have an intrinsic maximum. The "greatest possible number" that Plantinga invokes against Gaunilo in fact proves perfectly analogous here. For any natural number, there is a greater. For any body of knowledge, it appears—that possessed by any particular being, for example—there is some truth it leaves out and so some ideal body of knowledge beyond it. In chapter two this issue is broached in terms of Kaplan and Montague's paradox of the Knower. In chapter three it is raised with an eye to the Gödel results and related incompleteness phenomena using formal systems, and systems well beyond, as models of bodies of knowledge. One result here is that no such system is capable even of a *language* suitable for all truths.

Consider finally the opening lines of the *Tractatus*: "The world is the totality of facts." The suggestion that runs the length and breadth of the results I want to explore is that there ultimately *can* be no totality of facts. There can thus be no closed world of the form the *Tractatus* demands. If we think of the universe in terms of its truths, the universe itself, like any knowledge or description of it, is essentially open and incomplete.

Here caveats and provisos should of course be noted. What I've tried to sketch above is merely the general vision of the present study. Its strict conclusions, with crucial qualifications in place, appear embedded in the argument itself.

It must also be admitted that the attempt to draw philosophical lessons from metalogical texts is a notoriously perilous business. With that in mind, this work should perhaps be read with scholarly caution as an argument of interest, or a suggestion worthy of further work, rather than as an attempt at invincible proof. Scholarly caution can also be overstated, however. I consider much of the argument both powerful and compelling, and it is far from clear that philosophical argument should *ever* pretend to invincibility.

A further proviso is this. The work that follows clearly employs and relies on contemporary logic as we know it. Surely, there is no alternative. Nonetheless, conclusions throughout should perhaps be phrased so as to make that reliance explicit: *within any logic we have*, we should perhaps say, a totality of truths or a notion of total knowledge seems to prove incoherent.

What makes this an important rather than a trivial qualification is the fact that an air of paradox does pervade parts of the present study, and new logics have been developed in response to paradox before. The alternative reading this reflection offers for the study as a whole is explored briefly in the conclusion. Given any logic we have, I think, we are forced to abandon a range of basic philosophical preconceptions. But were the present study to stimulate development of new logical techniques instead— techniques revolutionary enough and powerful enough to leave it far behind—I would, of course, consider the work a great success.

Not all books are best read line by line, front cover to back. Here the simplicity and centrality of the Liar paradox demand that we start with the Liar, for example, but past work on the topic has been so extensive and so intricate that the first chapter then inevitably becomes a long one. A number of chapters, moreover, contain a technical core. With an eye to the general character of the argument as a whole, the reader is thus perhaps best advised to start with a reading that emphasizes the basic ideas of initial and concluding sections in each chapter, returning later for the finer details.

1 Apparent Lessons of the Liar

The Liar is perhaps the oldest and the deepest, as well as the simplest, of the paradoxes.[1] Here I want to start with the Liar because of its ideal simplicity. But one should not let that simplicity mislead; the conceptual difficulties that the Liar represents are genuinely profound ones, and the Liar itself can be seen to lie behind a range of the more technically sophisticated results considered in later chapters: the diagonal lemma, Cantorian arguments in general, and Gödel's theorems. To start with the Liar is to start with some of the deepest of conceptual problems in their simplest possible form.

In the first three sections that follow I want to introduce three particular Liar-like arguments: against a set of all truths, against a common approach to possible worlds, and against a notion of omniscience.

What these arguments *suggest* is that notions of a totality of truth or of total knowledge must prove incoherent. Here, as with more familiar forms of the Liar, it is, of course, tempting to look for a way out, and in sections 4 through 9, I consider a broad range of possible replies. The lessons of the Liar include the particular ways that such replies seem to fail.

1 Totality, Truth, and the Liar

Ordinary truths are familiar and easy to come by:

A book lies open before you.   (1)

Seven is a prime.   (2)

Our planet circles the sun.   (3)

Consider however truth in its totality, the totality of truths, the universe as a whole, as it were, conceived of in terms of its truths. Consider the set of all truths. *Is* there such a set? *Is* there what we imagine here, or what we imagine we imagine?

A set-theoretical form of the Liar seems to pose immediate problems for any such assumption. For suppose there *is* a set Θ of all truths, and consider

(4) is not a member of set Θ.   (4)

Is (4) a member of Θ or not? If it is *not* a member, it must be. For in that case (4) is true, since (4) asserts that it is not a member, and Θ is specified as including all truths. If (4) *is* a member, on the other hand, it must not be. For if (4) were a member of Θ, it would be false—(4) asserts that it is *not* a member. Since Θ includes only truths, Θ cannot include (4).

The assumption that there is a set of all truths leads to contradiction, then, whether we suppose (4) to be a member or not. What such a Liar-like argument *seems* to show, at least, is that there can be no set of all truths.[2]

Note that nothing in the argument here turns on sets in particular; we might have begun by imagining a collection or compendium or conglomerate of all truths instead, asking, for example, whether (5) is a constituent of a supposed conglomerate κ of all truths:

(5) is not a constituent of conglomerate κ.[3]   (5)

What this form of the Liar at least seems to offer, then, is an argument against *any* totality of truths.[4]

A number of responses are tempting, of course. But let me forestall those just long enough to introduce for discussion two similar Liar-like arguments.

2 Possible Worlds

On one common approach, as noted in the introduction, possible worlds are taken either to be, or to correspond to, maximal consistent sets of propositions. The *actual* world, on such an account, either is or corresponds to a maximal set of all truths.

Consider, for example, the outline of possible worlds given by Robert M. Adams:

The analysis which I have in mind is a reduction of talk about possible worlds to talk about sets of propositions.

Let us say that a *world-story* is a maximal consistent set of propositions. That is, it is a set which has as its members one member of every pair of mutually contradictory propositions, and which is such that it is possible that all of its members be true together. The notion of a possible world can be given a contextual analysis in terms of world-stories. Of the following statement forms, for example, (a), (c) and (e) are to be analyzed as equivalent to (b), (d), and (f), respectively.

There is a possible world in which *p*.   (a)

The proposition that (*p*) is a member of some world-story.   (b)

In every possible world, *q*.   (c)

The proposition that (q) is a member of every world-story. (d)

Let w be a possible world in which r. In w, t. (e)

Let s be a world-story of which the proposition that (r) is a member. The proposition that (t) is a member of s. (f)

A similar contextual analysis can now be given to the notion of actuality. "In the actual world, p" is to be analyzed as "The proposition that (p) is true." In accordance with this analysis, we can say that the actual world differs from the other possible worlds in that all the members of its world-story (the set of all the propositions that are true in it) are true. (Adams 1974, 225–226)[5]

Let us refer to that maximal consistent set of propositions in terms of which our world is specified on such an account—the maximal consistent set of propositions that constitute or correspond to the *actual* world—as A. Consider

(6) is not a member of set A. (6)

Were there a set A, of course, (6) would either be included as a member or would not. Here, as before, however, either alternative leads quite directly to contradiction. There can be no set of all truths, it appears, and thus there can be no world specified in terms of a set of all truths. In the sense of 'actual world' outlined in Adams' and other accounts, there can be no actual world.

Here the actual world is not the only victim, however. For suppose any possible world δ and a corresponding maximal consistent set D of all and only those propositions that would have obtained had δ been actual.[6] Will (7) be a member of set D or not?

(7) is not a member of D. (7)

Though somewhat complicated by modalities and conditionals, a Liar-like argument appears here as well. Suppose first that (7) *is* a member of D. Then had δ been actual, (7) would have obtained. But in that case (7), as (7) maintains, would *not* have been a member of D. Had δ been actual, in other words, (7) would not have obtained. Since D contains all and only propositions that would have obtained had δ been actual, (7) must *not* be a member of D.

Suppose, then, that (7) is not a member of D. Had δ been actual, (7) would not have obtained. Had δ been actual, in other words, (7) would not have been a member of the set of propositions that then obtained. Since D

is specified as precisely the set of propositions that would have obtained had δ been actual, (7) would not have been a member of D. But what (7) maintains is that it is not a member of D, so had δ been actual, (7) would have been *true*. Since D includes all propositions that would have obtained had δ been actual, it must be that (7) *is* a member of D.

The supposition of even a possible world corresponding to a maximal set of propositions, then, seems to lead to contradiction. On the outline of possible worlds offered above, it appears that there simply can be no possible worlds.

3   The Divine Liar

To qualify as omniscient, a being would have to believe all and only truths.[7] But it appears that there can be no such being. For suppose that there were an omniscient being, God, let us say, and consider a sentence we might term the Divine Liar:

God believes that (8) is false.   (8)

On the supposition that (8) is true, it is true that God believes that (8) is false. But we are supposing here that (8) is true, and thus we are forced to conclude that God holds a false belief. On such a supposition he cannot then qualify as omniscient.

On the supposition that (8) is false, it is not the case that God believes that (8) is false. But our supposition here is that (8) *is* false, and thus there must be a truth—that (8) is false—that God does not believe and hence does not know. Here again he fails to qualify as omniscient.

If (8) is either true or false, then, God is not omniscient. But, of course, God is not alone in this respect: a similar argument will hold for any being proposed as omniscient. It appears that there simply can be no omniscient being.[8]

Moreover, though the argument is phrased here in terms of a *single* omniscient being, this does not appear to be essential; a similar argument can be constructed against the supposed omniscience of any committee or consortium or any ultimate Peircean community of investigators.[9] Omniscience in general thus appears to be impossible. Or so the argument goes.

It should perhaps be emphasized that the hypothesis of omniscience *is* crucial for generating the contradiction above. For consider a sentence on the pattern of (8) but that concerns not God, or any other being supposed omniscient, but some mere epistemic mortal, Ralph Lingren, for example:

Ralph Lingren believes that (9) is false. (9)

Here we get no contradiction. If (9) is true, Ralph Lingren believes that it is false. Ralph must then hold a false belief. But since we know perfectly well that he's a mere mortal, this will give us no contradiction. If (9) is false, on the other hand, it is false that Ralph believes that (9) is false, and there is thus a truth that Ralph fails to believe. But here again, since Ralph has not been assumed to be omniscient, we get no contradiction.

Of course, (9) does have its own peculiarities from Ralph's perspective. Though *we* can consistently assign it a value of either true or false, it appears that he cannot. For suppose that Ralph believes that (9) is true. Since (9) maintains that Ralph believes that (9) is false, Ralph will then be able to see that (9) must be false. Given even minimal competence, then, Ralph will come to believe that (9) is false. But if he believes (9) to be false, since he can see that (9) maintains that he believes it to be false, he will be forced to conclude that (9) is true after all. Thus (9) is a personal paradox of sorts, custom monogrammed for Ralph Lingren.[10] On the other hand, (8) is something more. Given an assumption of omniscience, it leads to contradiction *simpliciter* and for all observers.

It should not come as a surprise, perhaps, that omniscience raises difficulties similar to those that face a totality of truths and a common approach to possible worlds. These are, after all, largely correlate notions. What would be known in omniscience is what would appear as a member of a set of all truths and what would obtain in an actual world as outlined; omniscience is merely the epistemic correlate to these. Viewed from the other side, these might be considered metaphysical instantiations of what would exist epistemically in omniscience. For every p, p would be an element of Θ and of A if and only if it were also a member of the set of beliefs B appropriate to an omniscient being. What Liar-like arguments *seem* to show is that none of these is coherent.

4 Possible Ways Out

The *apparent* lessons of the Liar, then, include the following: that there can be no totality of truths, that there can be no possible worlds conceived in terms of maximal consistent propositions, and that there can be no omniscient being. Here, as in the case of more standard versions of the Liar, one of course looks immediately for a way out. In the sections that follow, I want to consider a number of strategies in detail.

One approach, perhaps the obvious approach, is to deny the assumption relied on in all the arguments above that examples such as (4) through (8) *are* either true or false. Perhaps these must take some further value or be treated as lacking a truth-value altogether. Perhaps we can escape the apparent implications of Liar-like arguments by insisting that these are *neither* true nor false.

Allied with this first approach, but in some ways subtler and deeper, is a propositional response: that only propositions can properly be said to bear truth values and that the exhibited sentences fail to express propositions. Both the real strengths and the deep difficulties of an appeal to propositions have often gone unappreciated; in what follows, I try to offer a more complete and adequate treatment.

A third and more recent attempt has been to propose not that Liar-like sentences are *neither* true nor false but that they are *both* true *and* false—a postulation not of truth-value gaps but of truth-value gluts.

The most firmly entrenched responses to the Liar, and in many ways the most successful, involve appeals to hierarchy of one sort or another. In section 8, I concentrate on the classical hierarchies of Russell, Tarski, and Kripke, leaving consideration of a related account by Tyler Burge to chapter two.

In the final section I consider the elegant modeling of two approaches offered in Barwise and Etchemendy's recent book *The Liar* (1987). The implications of Barwise and Etchemendy's "Russellian" account are very much in line with my opening arguments; on such an account, the world itself fails to form a totality. An "Austinian" approach, on the contrary— so Barwise and Etchemendy claim—offers a solution to the Liar that salvages "virtually all our pretheoretic intuitions about truth and falsity" (164); in particular, "both the coherency and the totality of the world is preserved" (173). The real significance of such claims, I want to argue, calls for careful and critical scrutiny.

In the end, I want to suggest, none of these strategies proves adequate as a reply to the three arguments above. In a number of cases the strategies at issue simply prove inadequate against Liar-like difficulties in general. More interesting, however, are those responses that do seem to offer both deep insight into the structure of the Liar and more satisfying solutions, but not solutions that ultimately offer any hope for a totality of truths, for possible worlds as outlined, or for a notion of omniscience.

5   Truth-Value Gaps, Many-Valued Logics, and Strengthened Liars

Each of the arguments offered in preceding sections turns at some crucial point on the assumption that a Liar-like (4), (6), or (8) is either true or false. But perhaps this is simply a mistake. Perhaps these, along with the simple Liar,

(10) is false,   (10)

should be treated as *neither* true nor false.

Can one escape Liar-like arguments by proposing that such examples are neither true or false—that they carry some third value or constitute a third-value gap?[11] It appears not.

The standard obstacle to all such attempts is the Strengthened Liar. If we reject the simple Liar as neither true nor false, what then are we to say of

(11) is false or neither true nor false,   (11)

or simply

(12) is not true   ?   (12)

If (12) is true, of course, it is not. If it is either false or neither true nor false, on the other hand, it appears it must simply be true.

Essentially the same crucial difficulty for gapped and three-valued approaches is already built into the Liar-like arguments above.

Consider (8) again, for example. If (8) is neither true nor false, then God, specified as omniscient, knows that (8) is neither true nor false. It cannot be, then, that God believes that (8) is false. But (8) specifies that God *does* believe that (8) is false. So (8) must be false. If (8) is false, however, then it is not the case that God believes that (8) is false. Here as before there will be a truth that escapes God's notice—that (8) is false. Here as before we would have to concede that God—or any other being proposed in his place—is not omniscient.

As it stands, then, (8) has already the effect of a Strengthened Liar. The same applies to the other crucial sentences, and thus appeal to third values or truth-value gaps seems quite generally impotent as a response to the Liar-like arguments above.[12]

To explore many-valued logics and Strengthened Liars a bit more completely, let me make the discussion slightly more formal. Here I follow
Rescher in outlining many-valued logics in terms of a 'Vvp' operator that
assigns truth values to propositions about the truth value of propositions.
For any p, let $/p/$ indicate the value of p, and use 'Vvp' to indicate a
statement to the effect that p has the value v.[13]

The simple Liar, since it attributes the value F (for false) to itself, can be
represented as

$$VF(13),\tag{13}$$

which gives us $/(13)/ = /VF(13)/$.

Assumptions operative in the standard two-valued reasoning regarding
the Liar are reflected in the matrix given in table 1.1, which indicates, given
an asserted value v and an actual value of p, the value of a statement Vvp
to the effect that p has value v.

The familiar reasoning of the Liar now takes the following form: If
$/VF(13)/ = T$, then $/(13)/ = T$, by the identity above, and $/(13)/ = F$, by the
fact that $/VFF/ = F$ in the matrix above. [14] If $/VF(13)/ = F$, on the other
hand, then $/(13)/ = F$, by the identity above, and $/(13)/ = T$, by the fact that
$/VFF/ = T$ in the matrix.

Table 1.1
A two-valued matrix for Vvp

	p	
v	T	F
T	T	F
F	F	T

Table 1.2
A three-value matrix for Vvp

	p		
v	T	I	F
T	T	I	F
I	I	T	F
F	F	I	T

With just two values and the matrix in table 1.1 such an argument seems inescapable. But what if we introduce I as an additional option, thought of either as a third value or a truth-value gap? Consider, for example, the matrix in table 1.2 as a possible three-valued matrix for the Vvp operator.

Here as before, of course, $/(13)/ = /VF(13)/$. But in terms of this three-valued matrix, it no longer proves impossible to consistently assign (13) a value. Each of the self-referential statements (13),

$$VI(14), \tag{14}$$

and

$$VT(15) \tag{15}$$

can in fact consistently be assigned a value: I, F, and T respectively.[15]

A three-valued approach does then offer a response to the immediate difficulties of the simple Liar. As noted informally above, however, it will not prove adequate to address the deeper difficulties of the Strengthened Liar. More formally, consider

$$VF(16) \lor VI(16), \tag{16}$$

which gives us

$$/(16)/ = /VF(16) \lor VI(16)/.$$

Suppose that $/(16)/ = T$. Then $/VF(16) \lor VI(16)/ = /VFT \lor VIT/$, which by the matrix is $/F \lor I/$. By the identity above, $/(16)/ = /F \lor I/$.

Suppose that $/(16)/ = F$. Then $/VF(16) \lor VI(16)/ = /VFF \lor VIF/$, which by the matrix is $/T \lor F/$. If we read $/p \lor q/$ standardly as $\max[/p/, /q/]$, $/VF(16) \lor VI(16)/ = T$. So if $/(16)/ = F$, then also $/(16)/ = T$.

Suppose finally that $/(16)/ = I$. Then $/VF(16) \lor VI(16)/ = /VFI \lor VII/$, which by the matrix is $/F \lor T/$. If we again read $/p \lor q/$ as $\max[/p/, /q/]$, $/VF(16) \lor VI(16)/ = T$. If $/(16)/ = I$, then also $/(16)/ = T$.

As Rescher notes, to make these conclusions viable "we would be forced to the unpalatable expedient of having the truth table for '$\lor$' be such that $T = I \lor F$."[16]

Here I have technically shown the Strengthened Liar to pose difficulties for three-valued approaches only given a particular choice of three-valued Vvp matrix. Can't we substitute another matrix?

This proves an intriguing and informative question. Consider those features of the matrix on which the three-step argument above actually relies.

What the first step seems to demand is that for any value v, $/VvT/ = v$. This is reflected by the left column of the matrix; under a value of T for p, all values for Vvp reflect the v values to the left. In fact, even this isn't crucial, however. The first step above would have given us a similarly unpalatable conclusion as long as, for any value v such that $v = T$, $/VvT/ = T$. What the first step strictly requires, then, is simply that a value of T for $/VvT/$ is reserved solely for the case of VTT.

The crucial feature of our matrix on which the second and third steps of the argument rely is this: that for any value v, $/Vvv/ = T$. This is reflected by the fact that the diagonal from upper left to lower right in the matrix is a solid line of T's.

The argument above will hold, then—and the Strengthened Liar will create all the standard difficulties—for any three-valued Vvp matrix with these general features. These are not strictly necessary conditions on matrices; we could for example put values other than T on the diagonal. But such conditions do seem inescapable if 'T' is to reflect anything like a notion of truth.

The first condition on matrices amounts to this: only true statements are truly said to be true. The second condition amounts to the following: to say that a statement has the value it does is always to speak the truth. Any 'T' that did *not* fit these conditions would clearly be a dubious candidate for anything like truth.

We cannot technically say, then, that the Strengthened Liar will hold for all three-valued systems. But we can say that it will hold for any system with an ordinary disjunction $\lor$ such that $/p \lor q/ = \max[/p/, /q/]$ and in which 'T' retains even these minimal characteristics of truth. In that sense, escape from the Strengthened Liar by means of three-valued systems would demand not merely supplementing standard values but leaving genuine truth behind.[17]

I have so far dealt only with *three*-valued logics, however. Would the incorporation of still more values help? It should be fairly clear that the answer will be no.

For a four-valued system with values T, I_1, I_2, and F, we will be able to construct a slightly expanded form of the Strengthened Liar as follows:

$$VI_1(17) \lor VI_2(17) \lor VF(17) \tag{17}$$

This will give us the same results under the same general conditions: when the truth table for some connective '$\lor$' does the work of 'max' and the 'T'

of the matrix satisfies essential conditions on truth, appearing in the left column only at the top and in a solid line along the diagonal. As long as only true statements can truly be said to be true, and if to say that a statement has the value it does is always to speak the truth, the Strengthened Liar will remain.

Nor will the addition of finitely many more values escape these essential difficulties. For any system with T, F, and n intermediate I values I_1, I_2, I_3, ..., I_n, we will face a Strengthened Liar of the form

$$VI_1(18) \lor VI_2(18) \lor VI_3(18) \lor \ldots \lor VI_n(18) \lor VF(18). \tag{18}$$

What if we add an *infinite* number of additional values? Will *that* offer an escape? Rescher seems to think that it will, that here finally we'll find an escape from both the Liar and its strengthened kin:

For in such a logic, with numerical truth-values ranging from 0 to 1, inclusive, let:

$$Vvp = 1 - |v - /p/|$$

[where $|v - /p/|$ indicates the absolute difference between value v and the actual value of p.] Then the Liar paradox condition

$$(n) = Vv(n)$$

will *always* be solvable, since for every value of v there will always be a value u such that: $u = 1 - |v - u|$ or equivalently $|v - u| = 1 - u$. (The function $u = 1/2(1 + v)$ establishes the requisite relationship.)

Moreover, the negative Liar paradox condition

$$(m) = \sim Vv(m)$$

now requires that for every value v there is some value u such that:

$$u = /\sim Vvu/ = 1 - (1 - |v - u|)$$

$$u = |v - u|$$

But this can similarly be shown by noting that the function $u = 1/2v$ establishes the requisite relationship. Again, a statement of the form

$$(m) = [Vv(m) \lor Vv'(m)]$$

requires that for every v, v' there is a u such that:

$$u = /(1 - |v - u|) \lor (1 - |v' - u|)/$$

That this condition can always be satisfied (when, as usual, $/p \lor q/ = \max[/p/, /q/]$) can also be shown. Thus the various analogue versions of the Liar paradox all turn out to be nonparadoxical in the infinite-valued case. (Rescher 1969, 89–90)

Table 1.3
An infinite-valued matrix for *Vvp*

v	p								
	1	...	3/4	...	1/2	...	1/4	...	0
1	1	...	3/4	...	1/2	...	1/4	...	0
		1							
⋮	⋮	1							
			1						
3/4	3/4		1						1/4
				1					
⋮	⋮				1				⋮
1/2	1/2				1				1/2
						1			
⋮	⋮						1		⋮
1/4	1/4						1		3/4
								1	
⋮	⋮							1	⋮
									1
0	0	...	1/4	...	1/2	...	3/4	...	1

Despite Rescher's claim, however, even an infinite-valued logic will still face a form of the Strengthened Liar.

For the infinite-valued case, Rescher proposes that $/Vvp/ = 1 - |v - /p/|$, which gives us a matrix that we might envisage as in table 1.3. There each of an infinite number of points, plotted in the style of Cartesian coordinates from v and p axes, take on a value of $1 - |v - /p/|$. Despite its infinite values, the similarity of this matrix to those above should be clear.

Can we construct a Strengthened Liar for a system characterized by this matrix? Yes. Consider what we might term the Bionic Liar:

(19) has some value other than 1.   (19)

This we might envisage in any of various forms:

$/(20)/ \neq 1$,   (20)

$/(21)/ < 1$,   (21)

$\forall v[Vv(22) \rightarrow v = 1]$,   (22)

$$\forall v[Vv(23) \rightarrow v < 1]; \tag{23}$$

or as the infinite disjunction

$$Vv_1(24) \lor Vv_2(24) \lor Vv_3(24) \lor \ldots, \tag{24}$$

where $\{v_1, v_2, v_3, \ldots\}$ is the set of all values of the system other than 1.

Clearly, (19) through (24) are variations on a theme: in a universe of infinitely many values between 0 and 1, both '$\neq 1$' and '< 1' will amount to infinite disjunctions. For simplicity here, I will work directly in terms of the infinite disjunction.

What (24) gives us is

$$/(24)/ = /Vv_1(24) \lor Vv_2(24) \lor Vv_3(24) \lor \ldots /.$$

If we assign (24) a value of 1, its value will be equal to that of an infinite disjunction of Vvp statements with values v_1, v_2, $v_3, \ldots$, by the matrix above. But these were specified as precisely all values *other* than 1.

If we assign (24) a value v_n other than 1, on the other hand, somewhere within the infinite disjunction $Vv_1(24) \lor Vv_2(24) \lor Vv_3(24) \lor \ldots$ will appear a disjunct with the value of $Vv_n(v_n)$. By the matrix above, the value of that disjunct will be 1, and thus if '$\lor$' is still interpreted as doing the work of 'max', (24) will have a value of 1 after all.

To make this viable, to paraphrase Rescher, we would be forced to the unpalatable expedient of interpreting '$\lor$' so that $1 = v_1 \lor v_2 \lor v_3 \lor \ldots$ for some values $v_1, v_2, v_3, \ldots$, none of which equals 1.[18]

A form of the Strengthened Liar will then hold for infinite-valued logics as well. To defend the claim that "the various analogue versions of the Liar paradox all turn out to be unparadoxical in the infinite-valued case," we would apparently be forced to confine 'analogues' to *finite* disjunctions of the form of (18). But that would clearly be arbitrary and ad hoc—precisely as arbitrary as if we had denied that the original Strengthened Liar was an analogue of the simple Liar, on the ground perhaps that it was a complex rather than a simple statement. Such a restriction on the scope of 'analogues', at any rate, would do nothing to indicate that infinite-valued logics are in any way paradox-resistant.

The Bionic Liar, of course, requires powers of expression beyond those of its predecessors: infinite disjunction, '$\neq$', '$<$', or the like. But this was perhaps to be expected; the greater the 'n' of an n-valued logic, the greater power of expression is demanded in its Strengthened Liar. For a three-valued logic the Strengthened Liar requires only two-place disjunction, for example, whereas for a four-valued logic it requires three-place disjunction. It is also clear that an infinite-valued logic that lacks such forms of expression as those employed in (19) through (24) would be severely crippled —unable, for example, to express its own law of the excluded $(\omega + 1)$th.

The argument regarding infinite-valued logics above relies on the particular matrix Rescher suggests. But here as before, the basic assumptions at issue are minimal: that some connective will do the work of 'max' (here for the infinite case), that it will only be true (or '1') statements that can truly be said to be true, and that to say that a statement has the value it does is always to speak the truth. These conditions are reflected in the matrix in table 1.3 by the fact that '1' is reserved for only the highest point in the left column and by the fact that the descending diagonal is a solid line of 1's. Here as before, these characteristics of the matrix could be altered only at the cost of abandoning the notion that '1' or 'T' will represent anything like truth.

Many-valued logics in general, then, whether finite- or infinite-valued, seem powerless against forms of the Strengthened Liar. For essentially the same reasons, the appeal to many-valued logics will prove inadequate as a reply to Liar-like arguments regarding possible worlds, omniscience, and a totality of truths.

6   The Propositional Response

Crucial to the propositional response is a distinction between sentences on the one hand and a category of things they may be taken to express on the other.[19] Up to this point, it must be confessed, I have quite deliberately slurred any such distinction.

The following passage, for example, has been typical:

For suppose there *is* a set Θ of all truths, and consider

(4) is not a member of set Θ.   (4)

Is (4) a member of set Θ or not?

Here, of course, I employed a displayed sentence. Nonetheless, quite typically arguments have turned on '(4)', for example, being used to refer to a possible candidate for a truth or something known by an omniscient being. The essential strategy of the propositional response is to slip a deft knife between the sentences displayed in such contexts and the propositions they are taken to express: quasi-linguistic entities of some sort taken to be the *proper* objects of truth or knowledge.[20]

Consider first the virtues of a propositional approach with an eye to the Liar and the Strengthened Liar:

(10) is false.   (10)

(12) is not true.   (12)

The claim that (10) is either true or false, of course, leads to contradiction. The claim that (12) is true, false, or neither true nor false seems to lead to the same result. What a propositional account allows one to say, however, is that neither of these sentences expresses a proposition. That seems to be enough to effectively stop the line of argument crucial to presentations of both the Liar and its strengthened variations.

Let me first use numbers explicitly to refer to *sentences*. In that case, as long as one sticks to one's guns in maintaining that sentence (12) expresses no proposition, one can resist going on to say—as standard presentations often require—that (12) does have a truth value after all because of what "it says." If sentence (12) expresses no proposition, there simply *is* nothing that it says. We can then reject any supposed inference that (12) is true because it *says* it is not true and since it expresses no proposition, it is not true. On a propositional approach, there is nothing which either (10) or (12) or any other Liar-like sentence says, asserts, or maintains to be the case. All presentations of the Liar that rely at any point on a claim as to what the sentence at issue *says* are effectively blocked.[21]

The alternative is to try to use '(12)' to refer not to the sentence above but to a proposition it expresses. Here, however, the propositional strategy will take the form of directly challenging the assumption that there *is* any proposition expressed by the exhibited sentence and thus challenging the assumption that there is here any proposition to refer to.

A similar propositional strategy will, of course, be applicable to the Liar-like arguments of earlier sections. In each case the argument turns at some point on a pattern of reasoning like the following: If (8) is neither true nor false, it cannot be that God believes that (8) is false. But (8) specifies that God *does* believe that (8) is false. So (8) must be false.

However, if we take '(8)' as a reference to the exhibited sentence and insist that that sentence expresses no proposition, there *is* nothing that it says or specifies. The inference that (8) is false after all because of what it *says* can then be effectively blocked. The attempt to take '(8)' as a reference to a particular *proposition* can similarly be rejected: the argument then hangs on the assumption that the exhibited sentence does express some proposition capable of being referred to, and that assumption the propositionalist can be expected to deny.

With regard to Liar-like arguments in general, a propositional approach has much to recommend it. Indeed, its effectiveness against various forms of the Liar is perhaps the strongest argument we *have* in favor of a doctrine of propositions. Nonetheless, such an approach carries a number of major vices as well.

Perhaps the most familiar charge leveled against propositions, in the Quinean tradition in particular, is the claim that they are children of darkness, obscure and dubiously intelligible. What, after all, could propositions *be*? And how could such things, if things they be, be either identified or individuated?

The force of that critique is perhaps not what it once was, simply because serious attempts *have* been made to construct formal theories of properties and propositions that do, for example, include criteria of propositional identity (see, for example, Bealer 1982, Turner 1987, and Zalta 1983). Though the limitations of such accounts leave it far from clear that their notions of propositions can serve the purposes demanded here, and though a significant challenge remains to construct a coherent account that does justice to the full range of informal intuitions, it's probably true that the work that has been done does blunt any simple rejection of propositions as essentially and inherently unintelligible.[22]

There are other vices of a propositionalist approach that prove more serious, however. One is that a propositional approach is in some ways too *easy* a reply to the Liar and its kin, at least with regard to some of the questions that many who have taken on the Liar have tried to answer. Surely it is not enough merely to *say* that sentence (4) or (6) or (7) or (8) doesn't express a proposition, for we will also want to know *why*. What is it about such sentences that keeps them from expressing a proposition or deprives them of a proposition to express? A propositional account alone offers no theory of *why* certain sentences will supposedly fail to express propositions, and in that sense, it seems too *thin* to qualify as a satisfactory solution.[23]

Here we can also draw a lesson, I think, from the experience of a different tradition with regard to the Liar. One approach in terms of sentences has been to attempt to formulate explicit constraints on the range of sentences over which 'true' and 'false' would be allowed to apply. The inevitable challenge that has faced such attempts has been effectively to exclude the Liar and all troublesome variations and yet at the same time not to exclude apparently innocuous forms of self-reference or fundamental theorems of, say, set theory and recursion theory. The perennial sorrow of such attempts has been that they either exclude the unforgivable or fall victim to a form of the Strengthened Liar formulated in terms of their own categories.[24] A propositional account alone, as noted, gives us no general theory of *why* certain sentences will supposedly fail to express propositions. But it appears that any supplementary theory designed to fill this need would have to sort sentences in precisely the manner of the sentential approach and thus would require all the complexities and would face all the problems of that approach.[25]

Here, however, I want to press a further difficulty—that of the Propositional Liar:

(25) expresses no true proposition.   (25)

Is (25) true or false? If true, one might initially argue, it must be false, for (25) itself maintains that it is *not* true. If false, on the other hand, it must be true—or so the argument goes—for then, as (25) maintains, it expresses no true proposition. It might be proposed as a third alternative that (25) is neither true nor false. But if neither true nor false, it is in particular not true—it expresses no true proposition. Since all that (25) *says* is that it expresses no true proposition, it must be true after all.

A propositionalist can, of course, be expected to block this pattern of reasoning by insisting that the exhibited sentence simply expresses no proposition. In the case of the Propositional Liar, however, such a strategy becomes very awkward indeed.

The propositionalist's *solution* is to say that sentence (25) expresses no proposition. The partisan of propositions must hold, then, that sentence (26) *does* express a true proposition despite the fact that (25) and (26) are identical word for word and differ only in their clerical numbering.[26]

(25) expresses no true proposition.   (26)

A propositionalist is not forced at this point to say that sentence (25) is true after all, on the grounds that (26) is true and says just what (25) says. The consistent propositionalist *is* forced to maintain, however, that despite all appearances there is all the difference in the world between (25) and (26). Sentence (25) expresses no proposition, and so, of course, carries no truth value. Sentence (26), on the other hand, though identical word for word, does express a proposition, and moreover expresses a truth. Sentence (25) poses a problem and on a propositional account is to be rejected as propositionally subpar. Sentence (26), identical word for word, is an easy entailment from the propositional *solution*.

This is not strictly an inconsistent position, I think. But that hardly makes it a comfortable one; it simply does not seem that there can be as great a difference between (25) and (26) as the propositionalist is forced to claim. There are also closely related difficulties here. Identical referring expressions in (25) and (26) seem to have the same reference, and nonreferring expressions seem to have the same sense. How is that to be reconciled, on a propositional account, with the apparent truism that what is expressed by a sentence is entirely determined by the reference and sense of referring and nonreferring terms respectively?[27]

The propositionalist defender of a set Θ of all truths, of set-theoretic possible worlds, or of omniscience will face similar difficulties. Consider, for example, sentence (27):

God believes that (27) expresses no true proposition.   (27)

By a standard Liar-like argument, the claim that (27) is true, false, or neither true nor false will lead to contradiction. The propositionalist defender of omniscience can, of course, be expected to attempt to block such an argument by insisting that (27) expresses no proposition. If so, however, it clearly expresses no true proposition, and God, since he believes all truths, will believe that (27) expresses no true proposition. The propositionalist defender of omniscience will then have to hold that sentence (28) does express a true proposition, while also maintaining that sentence (27), identical word for word, expresses no proposition at all.

God believes that (27) expresses no true proposition.   (28)

We can also make the propositionalist's predicament still more telling. For consider the following sentence schemata:

If p, then (29) expresses no true proposition, and
if $\sim p$, then (30) expresses no true proposition.   (29)

If p, then (29) expresses no true proposition, and
if $\sim p$, then (30) expresses no true proposition.   (30)

Pick any p such that p or $\sim p$, and consider the resultant pair of sentences (29) and (30). These will, of course, be identical word for word. But consider what a propositionalist will have to say according to whether p or $\sim p$ in fact obtains.

If p obtains, (29) will lead to difficulty in precisely the manner of (25). For if p is the case, the second conjunct of (29) will be satisfied in virtue of a false antecedent. The truth value of (29) will then depend on the truth value of its first conjunct alone, and since p is the case, that truth value will be determined by the value of '(29) expresses no true proposition'. On the assumption that p obtains, in other words, (29) simply amounts to '(29) expresses no true proposition', a simple variant of (25).

On a propositionalist strategy, of course, we will then say that (29) expresses no proposition. If so, it expresses no true proposition, and thus the first conjunct of (30) will be true. On the assumption that p obtains, the second conjunct of (30) is assured in virtue of a false antecedent. Given p, then, on a propositional account, (30) will express a true proposition, and (29) no proposition at all.

On the other hand, if p does not obtain—if $\sim p$—the roles of (29) and (30) will be reversed. The first conjunct of (30) will now be satisfied in virtue of a false antecedent, and the value of (30) will thus depend on its second conjunct alone. That in turn will depend on the value of '(30) expresses no true proposition', and here (30) will amount to a simple variant of (25).

Given $\sim p$, then, it will be (30) that expresses no proposition. If so, it will express no true proposition, and thus the first conjunct of (29) will be true. The second conjunct of (29) is assured in virtue of a false antecedent. If p does not obtain, then, it will be (29) that expresses a true proposition and (30) that expresses no proposition at all.

The general lesson here is this. Given any p such that p or $\sim p$, there will be two sentences identical word for word, differing only in their clerical numbering, and such that on a propositional account, one expresses a true proposition and the other expresses no proposition at all. In order to tell which is which, however, we would have to know whether or not p in fact obtains.

One consequence of a propositional account is thus that the propositional status of sentences—whether a sentence does or does not express a proposition—will often prove inscrutable. To distinguish the propositional from the nonpropositional in *all* pairs of sentences such as (29) and (30), we would have to know, for *all* p, whether p or $\sim p$. To be able to distinguish proposition-expressing sentences from propositionless sentences in all cases, *we would have to know all truths*—a peculiar twist indeed for an argument one target of which is omniscience.

By the same token, were we somehow in a position to distinguish the propositional from the nonpropositional in all cases, that alone would allow us to infer any truth whatsoever. For in order to tell whether p or $\sim p$ is the case for any p—whether Goldbach's conjecture is correct or time travel is possible or the human race will survive the twenty-first century— we would need only to frame sentences on the pattern of (29) and (30) and examine them for propositional status. If it is (30) that expresses a proposition, p is the case; if it is (29), p is not the case. On a propositional account, then, any individual able to distinguish the propositional from the non-propositional in all cases would constitute an infallible oracle.[28]

Let me finally press a Quinean form of the Propositional Liar. Consider the following:

'Appended to its own quotation does not express a true proposition' appended to its own quotation does not express a true proposition.

To avoid contradiction, of course, a propositionalist will have to say that this does not express a proposition. The propositional solution might then be put as follows:

'Appended to its own quotation does not express a true proposition' appended to its own quotation does not express a proposition.

Whatever expresses no proposition at all, of course, expresses no true proposition. So,

'Appended to its own quotation does not express a true proposition' appended to its own quotation does not express a true proposition.

This last simple entailment from the propositional solution, however, is precisely the problem it was designed to solve.

Here we may come closest to squeezing an explicit contradiction from the propositional approach. The propositionalist must maintain that his solution is true, and thus that anything entailed by his solution is true. But if the propositional solution is true, at least one entailment, that exhibited above, will fail to express a proposition. It will then be neither true nor false, and thus in particular, it will *not* be true.

What might the propositionalist say here? In similar cases considered above, the propositionalist was able to maintain consistency—though perhaps mere consistency and perhaps consistency at an unacceptable cost—by insisting, for example, that sentence (26) expresses a true proposition whereas (25) expresses no proposition at all. To pursue that same strategy here, the propositionalist would have to say that the exhibited sentence with which we began,

'Appended to its own quotation does not express a true proposition' appended to its own quotation does not express a true proposition,

expresses *no* proposition, on the model of (25). However, the entailment from the propositional solution,

'Appended to its own quotation does not express a true proposition' appended to its own quotation does not express a true proposition,

must express a *true* proposition, on the model of (26).

Using (25) and (26) as a model, it thus appears that the propositionalist must claim at the very least that the exhibited entailment is not self-referential in the same sense that the initial displayed sentence is—as perhaps (26) is not self-referential in the same sense that (25) is. But to argue that the exhibited entailment is not fully self-referential, one would have to argue that it is not 'Appended to its own quotation does not express a true proposition' appended to its own quotation. A hard brief indeed, for that, it appears, is empirically false.

The propositional approach, it must be admitted, does seem initially attractive as a possible reply to the Liar and Liar-like arguments. Some of the problems traditionally leveled against such an approach, moreover, can be taken less as critiques than as challenges to the propositionalist to develop a more explicit and complete account. Other difficulties, however, including those that cluster around the Propositional Liar, go significantly deeper. These seem to indicate profound and pervasive flaws in the strategy itself.

7 Accepting Inconsistency

It has recently been proposed by a number of philosophers that the Liar and its kin not be rejected as *neither* true nor false—the approach considered in section 5—but accepted as *both* true *and* false. Graham Priest, for example, suggests that "trying to solve the paradoxes may be the wrong thing to do. Suppose we stop banging our heads against a brick wall trying to find a solution, and accept the paradoxes as brute facts. That is, some sentences are true (and true only), some false (and false only), and some both true and false!"[29]

Proponents of such a view are quick to try to disarm the objection that given an explicit contradiction, one can deduce any conclusion whatsoever. The classical argument, of course, is that given p and $\sim p$, we can deduce any q as follows:

p

$p \vee q$ addition

$\sim p$

q disjunctive syllogism

If certain principles of classical logic are sacrificed, however, such a derivation can be blocked. A variety of paraconsistent logics have been developed in which isolated contradictions can be quarantined and general triviality avoided.[30]

Despite the significant technical interest of such formal attempts, however, the proposal that we simply embrace contradiction must be treated as a counsel of despair. How great a counsel of despair will depend on the particular form of the proposal at issue.

Nicholas Rescher and Robert Brandom have outlined an approach in which, by means of aberrant worlds in a nonstandard ontology and a nonstandard semantics, isolated contradictions can be quarantined without any modification of classical logic. Consistency is effectively maintained on a higher level.[31] But in the end, such an approach does not prove adequate as a response to Liar-like difficulties in general. It still falls victim to the Strengthened Liar, for example, and Rescher and Brandom are forced to conclude, "The availability of non-standard worlds does not itself automatically resolve all of the difficulties posed by semantical paradoxes."[32]

Graham Priest's approach is significantly bolder and *is* intended as a response to Liar-like difficulties in general. But his approach is also in the end significantly more costly.

Priest explicitly rejects Rescher and Brandom's attempt to maintain consistency on a higher level: "This approach is too half-hearted to be workable. For it retains the object-language/meta-language distinction.... Once the object/meta-language distinction has collapsed it follows that we have no reason to expect our own semantic discussions to be consistent. Indeed, we have every reason to expect them not to be" (Priest 1984, 160–161). The result is a bewildering flurry of paradoxical implications. Priest must ultimately say not only that sentence (31), for example, is both true and false but that it is both true and false and *not* both true and false, both paradoxical and not paradoxical.[33]

This sentence is not true.   (31)

Sentence (32) will be both true only and not true only.

This sentence is not true only.   (32)

On such an approach the following will both be true:

All sentences are either true or false.   (33)

Some sentences are neither true nor false.   (34)

And in the end even (35), the apparent denial of Priest's position, will come out true.

No sentence is both true and false.[34]   (35)

   In Rescher and Brandom's approach, contradiction is closely confined, with consistency maintained on a higher level. Within Priest's approach, inconsistency seems to run rampant. But surely it must be admitted in either case that contradiction *is* an evil to be avoided. As advocates of inconsistency-tolerant systems have standardly argued, we *may* be forced to accept contradiction when there is no alternative. But in the Liar-like arguments here at issue, there clearly *is* an alternative: we can abandon notions of a set of all truths, of set-theoretic possible worlds, and of omniscience.

   What contradictory beliefs guarantee us, after all, is *false* beliefs. Contradiction is the short road to falsehood, and if *falsehood* is not to be avoided, it's not clear what is. In a way, even those who most vociferously urge us to accept contradiction seem to concede this point, for even they reject with horror the prospect of a trivial system in which *anything* follows. But what is wrong with triviality if not that it assures that even falsehoods will appear as theorems?

   If contradiction is to be avoided whenever possible, as surely it is, then proposals that we gracefully embrace contradiction are to be rejected whenever possible as well. As Aristotle notes, it is *most* true that two contradictory judgments cannot *both* be true.

8   The Appeal to Hierarchy

None of the approaches to Liar-like arguments surveyed in previous sections seems to prove satisfactory. Neither truth-value gaps nor truth-value gluts, neither appeals to propositions nor many-valued logics, seem to offer any adequate escape. But we have yet to address what may be the strongest response to the Liar: an appeal to hierarchy. Here I concentrate on Russell, Tarski, and Kripke, leaving to chapter two a similar treatment of a related account by Tyler Burge.

What I want to argue is the following: that whatever the virtues of a hierarchical response to the Liar, it does nothing to blunt the force of the arguments with which we began. For whatever its virtues in other regards, a hierarchical approach prohibits precisely the global notions of truth and knowledge that these would demand. Hierarchy of one form or another has a great deal in its favor as an attractive escape from the Liar. But a necessary cost of that escape seems to be abandonment of a set of all truths, of set-theoretic possible worlds, and of a notion of omniscience.

Russell

The set-theoretic problem now known as Russell's paradox concerns a set S defined as the set of all sets that are not members of themselves: $\{x \mid x \notin x\}$. The assumption that S either is a member of itself or is not leads, of course, to contradiction.

Russell's response to the paradox in *The Principles of Mathematics* is the simple theory of types. Here the objects of the universe are divided into an ascending hierarchy of individuals (type 0), classes of individuals (type 1), classes of classes of individuals (type 2), and so on. All variables are in effect subscripted according to type: variable x_0 will range over objects of type 0, x_1 over objects of type 1, and so forth. Expressions of the form '$x \in y$' are admitted as significant only when y carries a subscript one higher than that of x.[35]

The application to Russell's paradox should be clear; given any uniform subscript on x, both '$x \in x$' and '$x \notin x$' will be rejected as meaningless. The purported definition of set S above can then be dismissed as simply ill formed.

The simple theory of types, however, does not prove adequate against the broader range of "semantic" paradoxes, including the Liar and its kin. In "Mathematical Logic as Based on the Theory of Types" (1908) and *Prinicipia Mathematica* (1910) Russell therefore offers a richer ramified theory in which the basic pattern is elaborated in terms of orders of propositional functions and indeed types within orders.

For our purposes here, the important feature of the ramified theory is simply that it divides propositions into a hierarchy of orders. Roughly, propositions merely about individuals—those with no quantification over propositional variables—will be *first-order* propositions. Propositions about first-order propositions—those with quantification over first-order propositional variables but no higher—will be *second-order* propositions, and so forth. Each significant proposition will thus be assigned a single order, and no proposition about propositions of equal or higher order will be admitted as significant. In the terminology of "Mathematical Logic as Based on the Theory of Types," propositions of order n will contain propositions of order $n - 1$, but no higher, as apparent variables.[36]

Clearly, the Liar in any of its forms will be excluded as meaningless on such an account. In order for (10) to pose the standard difficulties, for example, it must be read as significantly asserting its own falsehood. The ramified theory of types, however, neatly prohibits such a reading. Every significant proposition must carry one and only one order type. But if (10) were assigned any order type n, on the Liar-like reading required, it would also have to be assigned the order type $n + 1$, on the grounds that it is *about* a proposition of order n. So (10) and all other forms of the Liar will simply find no place in a Russellian hierarchy of significant propositions.

When a man says "I am lying" we must interpret him as meaning: "There is a proposition of order n which I affirm and which is false." This is a proposition of order $n + 1$; hence the man is not affirming any proposition of order n; hence his statement is false, and yet its falsehood does not imply, as that of "I am lying" appeared to do, that he is making a true statement. This solves the Liar. (Russell 1908, 166)

The pure ramified theory of types brings with it significant technical difficulties, however. Within its confines, identity cannot be defined, and it becomes impossible to prove important bound theorems in analysis. Cantorian infinities crucial to so much of modern mathematics are blocked, and even the principle of mathematical induction must be abandoned in full generality.[37] To compensate for such difficulties, Russell introduces an axiom of reducibility, but it is not clear that such an addition isn't ad hoc or worse. Quine, for example, charges, "The axiom of reducibility is self-effacing: if it is true, the ramification it is meant to cope with was pointless to begin with" (1967, 152).

More significant for our purposes here, however, is a much less subtle limitation of the theory of types. For given the restrictions of a Russellian hierarchy, it clearly becomes impossible even to *state* (36) or other fundamental principles.

Every proposition is either true or false.   (36)

No significant proposition regarding *all* propositions can in fact be expressed at all. For if (36), for example, is about propositions of *all* orders, as intended, it can itself be assigned no order and so cannot qualify as significant. It is far from clear, for that matter, whether Russell's theory of types itself can be significantly stated within the confines of its own strictures.

By the same token, on a theory of types, there can be no truths about *all* truths. Consider, for example, the following:

Set Θ is the set of all truths.   (37)

A contains all actual truths.   (38)

God knows all truths.   (39)

If significant, each of these must belong to a propositional order higher than that of any proposition they are about. But if about all truths, as intended, they must have an order higher than that of any truth and thus cannot themselves be true.

On a theory of types, there simply can be no truth regarding all truths. But given a maximal consistent set A of all truths corresponding to an actual world, a set Θ of all truths, or an omniscient being, there surely *would* be truths regarding all truths: that all truths belong to A, belong to Θ, or are known by an omniscient being, for example. Given a Russellian hierarchy, then, it appears that there can be no set A, no set of all truths, and no omniscient being.

None of this should perhaps be surprising. It certainly would have been no surprise to Russell. For the guiding principle of the theories of types, simple and ramified, is the "vicious circle principle." In one form, "If, provided a certain collection had a total, it would have members only definable in terms of that total, then the said collection has no total" (Russell 1908, 155).[38] If truths did have a total—say in the form of a set Θ of all truths, a maximal consistent set A corresponding to the actual world, or the knowledge of an omniscient being—there *would* be truths "only definable in terms of" that total: truths about A, for example, or about such an omniscient being. On the vicious circle principle alone, then, as on its instantiation in a Russellian theory of types, there simply can be no such totalities of truth.[39]

Tarski

Tarski, very much in Russell's footsteps, proposes a hierarchy of languages $L_0, L_1, L_2, \ldots$, each language of which contains the truth predicate for the language below it in the hierarchy. In place of a single predicate 'true', then, we have an ascending series of predicates 'true-in-L_0', 'true-in-L_1', 'true-in-L_2', ..., which we might alternatively envisage as an ascending series of subscripted predicates 'true$_0$', 'true$_1$', 'true$_2$',....[40]

Though it is here technically sentences rather than propositions that are at stake, the essential hierarchical strategy remains the same. If 'true' is permitted to appear only with a subscript, and if a truth predicate 'true$_n$' is allowed to apply only to sentences involving a truth predicate of subscript less than n, the Liar sentence becomes simply ungrammatical. Its truth predicate requires some subscript n, but on the interpretation required for paradox, that predicate is then applied to the Liar sentence itself, in violation of explicit restrictions.

A similar hierarchical strategy could clearly be applied to the Liar-like arguments of previous sections. In the case of the Divine Liar, for example, we might propose either a Tarskian hierarchy of truth predicates within belief contexts or a hierarchy for predications of divine belief.[41] In the case of (4),

$$\text{(4) is not a member of set } \Theta, \tag{4}$$

we might similarly insist that predications of membership be indexed and restricted hierarchically, at least where sets of truths are at issue.

In a number of important respects, the Tarskian hierarchy is an improvement over Russell's theory of types. Here no aspects of classical mathematics are threatened in a way that calls for any analogue of the axiom of reducibility, for example.[42] But a Tarskian hierarchy still does not come without significant cost. It is technically limited to finite levels, those levels are fixed intrinsically and in advance rather than floating on wayward facts as forms of the Liar often do, and it is unable to deal intuitively with cases in which Richard Nixon and John Dean call each other liars.[43]

Here, however, I want to press two simpler objections. The first—a difficulty also in Russell and a lingering problem for hierarchial treatments throughout—is that appeal to hierarchy appears ad hoc. Familiar notions of truth, belief, membership, and the like simply don't seem to come with anything like subscripts attached, and thus hierarchical replies characteristically have the air of clever technical impositions rather than intuitively motivated and satisfying solutions.

Second and for my purposes more important, a Tarskian hierarchy effectively prohibits any global notion of truth or knowledge. Once 'true' is replaced by an infinitely fragmented series of truth predicates, '$true_0$', '$true_1$', '$true_2$',..., for example, we are left without any grammatical way even to state (40) or other basic logical laws.

Every sentence is true or false. (40)

If, as intended, (40) is about sentences at *all* hierarchical levels, neither its truth predicate nor any truth predicate applied to it could be assigned *any* level. Were we to adopt a similar hierarchical treatment for levels of divine knowledge or for truth in belief contexts, neither the relevant predicate of any true (41) nor of the claim that God believes that (41) is true could be assigned any level.

God believes all truths. (41)

Were membership in sets of truths indexed as suggested above, the predicate of any true (42) could similarly be assigned no hierarchical level.

All truths are members of Θ. (42)

On a Tarskian hierarchy, neither notions of omniscience, a set of all truths, nor a maximal consistent set A corresponding to the actual world can be specified at all. As a definition for omniscience, for example, we might suggest

A being x is *omniscient* $=_{df}$ for all p, p is true iff x believes that p AND x believes that p iff x knows that p.[44] (43)

But if, as intended, 'for all p' here is to include the substance of (43) as well, it is impossible to assign 'true' as it appears in the definition any hierarchical level. Set Θ might be specified as follows:

$$\forall p(p \in \Theta \text{ iff } p \text{ is true}) \tag{44}$$

But for any subscript n that we might attach to 'true' here, Θ will fail to include the truth that (44) itself is intended to express.

Moreover, this feature of a Tarskian hierarchy—an effective prohibition of any global notion of truth or knowledge—is far from accidental. The very purpose of a hierarchical strategy, after all, is precisely to prohibit such global notions. Were we to keep Tarskian levels but to reintroduce a global truth predicate, for example, Liar-like difficulties would return. A Global Liar might take the form of

$$\text{(45) is not globally true.} \tag{45}$$

If (45) is globally true, it is true on all levels that there is some level on which (45) is not true. Given any level on which (45) is not true, however, it appears it will simply be true.

Kripke

One response to the Liar, we've seen, is the invocation of a third truth value or the option of none: 'neither true nor false'. Another is appeal to a Tarskian hierarchy. What Kripke does is to combine these in a technically sophisticated and ingenious way.[45]

Truth for Kripke, unlike for Tarski, will be only partially defined. Those sentences not assigned truth values are termed *ungrounded*, and it is this crucial notion of groundedness that is technically specified in terms of a hierarchy of languages.

"Suppose," Kripke says, "we are explaining the word 'true' to someone who does not yet understand it" (Kripke 1975, 701). We might do so by means of the following principle:

One may assert that a sentence is true just when one is entitled to assert that sentence, and one may assert that it is not true just when one is entitled to deny it.

The learner, let us assume, starts off entitled to assert 'Snow is white' and the like and thus, by the principle above, '"Snow is white" is true'. Repeated applications of the principle allow iterations of 'is true', and using existential generalization and other statements, we can envisage him eventually capable of handling, say, 'Some sentence printed in the *New York Times* is true'.

> In this manner, the subject will eventually be able to attribute truth to more and more sentences involving the notion of truth itself. There is no reason to suppose that *all* statements involving 'true' will become decided in this way, but most will. Indeed, our suggestion is that the 'grounded' sentences can be characterized as those which eventually get a truth value in the process. (Kripke 1975, 701)

Somewhat more technically, though I simplify, the approach is as follows. One introduces a hierarchy of languages beginning with L_0, L_1, $L_2,\ldots$, and '$T(x)$' is interpreted within any language $L_{\alpha+1}$ as the truth predicate for sentences of L_α, much as before. At the lowest level L_0, then, '$T(x)$' is completely undefined. At L_1 it is assigned to wffs that do not themselves contain '$T(x)$', and so on, precisely in line with the intuitive sketch above.[46] At each stage wffs previously assigned truth values retain them, but definite truth values are also assigned to new wffs for which '$T(x)$' was previously undefined. In that sense '$T(x)$' becomes more defined as the process continues.[47]

A nice technical aspect of the Kripkean approach is that after sufficiently many stages, indeed, transfinitely many, the process saturates at a fixed point; the sets of true and false sentences are the same as at the preceding level.[48] A wff will be said to be *grounded* just in case it is assigned a truth value at the smallest fixed point. Among those sentences not grounded will be

(10) is false   (10)

(46) is true.   (46)

A Kripkean hierarchy of this sort has a number of advantages over the classical Tarskian approach. It is specified beyond finite levels, it can intuitively handle cases in which Nixon and Dean call each other liars, and it is consistent with allowing the level of sentences to float on empirical facts.

There are also phenomena that it does not seem capable of handling, however. Consider, for example, a pattern of reasoning regarding the following three sentences, adapted from Gupta 1982 via Barwise and Etchemendy 1987:

(49) is true.   (47)

(49) is false.   (48)

(47) is false or (48) is false.   (49)

Number (48) is false, so the reasoning goes. For suppose it were true. Then (49) would be false, and hence both its disjuncts would be false. But in that case it would be false that (47) is false; (47) would be true, and thus (49) would be true, which gives us a contradiction. Since (48) is false, then, (49) will be true, and thus (47) will be true as well.

The force of this pattern of reasoning, though clearly intuitive, is incapable of being captured within the Kripkean approach. For at no point in the Kripkean construction will any of these be assigned a truth value; each of these, like (10) and (46), will simply be ungrounded.

More important for my purposes here, however, is another limitation regarding the Kripkean account: the fact that despite initial appearances, it ultimately forces us to a pattern of ascending metalanguages on precisely the Tarskian pattern.

Kripke's answer to the Liar is essentially that of any three-valued approach: that (10) is neither true nor false but ungrounded. But what then of a Strengthened Liar,

(50) is false or ungrounded.   (50)

or simply (12)?

(12) is not true.   (12)

Surprisingly, Kripke does not directly address the issue of the Strengthened Liar. But his response would evidently be that 'true' as it appears in (12), as well as 'ungrounded' in (50), must be treated as predicates of a further metalanguage:

Liar sentences are *not true* in the object language, in the sense that the inductive process never makes them true; but we are precluded from saying this in the object language by our interpretation of negation and the truth predicate.... The necessity to ascend to a metalanguage may be one of the weaknesses of the present theory. (Kripke 1975, 714)

If the predicates of (50) and (12) are consigned to a metalanguage, the Strengthened Liar will, of course, have no grammatical place within Kripke's original hierarchy of languages, just as the standard Liar has no grammatical place within the Tarskian hierarchy. We now have two senses of 'true', however. Let us write the 'true' of (12), exiled to the metalanguage, as 'true$_m$'. We can remind ourselves that 'ungrounded' is also a purely metalinguistic predicate by writing it 'ungrounded$_m$'.

What then of (51)?

(51) is not true$_m$.   (51)

This clearly cannot be a sentence of the original hierarchy, since it contains an explicitly metalinguistic predicate. But if taken as a sentence of the metalanguage, is (28) true or untrue in the metalinguistic sense? Paradox will return for any 'true'-like construal of 'true$_m$'. For if (51) is true$_m$, it appears, it is not true$_m$. If it is not true$_m$, it must be true$_m$.[49]

One option here is to reject (51) as a sentence of the metalanguage, on the grounds that a sentence of linguistic level m cannot be assigned a truth predicate of level m. This is, of course, precisely the Tarskian strategy with regard to the Liar. Statements of our metalanguage can still be said to be true or false, but only in terms of a meta-metalinguistic predicate 'true$_{m'}$'.

Another option is to accept (51) as a sentence of the metalanguage but to treat it as an *ungrounded* sentence. Groundedness and ungroundedness within the metalanguage might in fact be treated in terms of ascension to a fixed point, much as in Kripke's original hierarchy. But, of course, (51) could not be said to be ungrounded$_m$ or not true$_m$. Short of paradox, we would have to say perhaps that (51) is ungrounded$_{m'}$ or not true$_{m'}$, using the distinct groundedness and truth predicates of a further meta-metalanguage.

Either option here clearly leads to an ascending series of metalanguages with distinct truth predicates on precisely the Tarskian model. Kripke's comment that "the ghost of the Tarskian hierarchy is still with us" (1975, 714) thus seems a serious understatement.

A Kripkean approach, like a Tarskian one, will also effectively prohibit any global notion of truth or knowledge. Here again, perhaps despite initial appearances, truth will be infinitely fragmented into metalinguistic levels. We will thus again have no grammatical way even to *state*, for example,

Every sentence is true or false.   (40)

Any statement regarding all truths will similarly have no metalanguage to call home. Within a Kripkean hierarchy, as within its predecessors, there will be neither any way to coherently specify a set Θ of all truths nor a way to characterize any being as omniscient.

In the end, the hierarchical approach is arguably the most compelling treatment of the Liar we have. Unlike gapped and many-valued responses, appeal to hierarchy does seem genuinely adequate against strengthened as well as simple forms of the Liar, yet it avoids both the fatal perplexities of propositions and the dubious attractions of contradiction. As is clear in Russell, Tarski, and Kripke, however, the hierarchical approach leaves no place for a set Θ of all truths, an actual world corresponding to a maximal truth set A, or a notion of omniscience.[50] In the end, such an approach thus confirms rather than challenges the conclusions of the Liar-like arguments with which we began.

9 Barwise and Etchemendy

A recent and significant addition to the literature is Jon Barwise and John Etchemendy's *The Liar* (1987), in which they offer formal models for both an "Austinian" and a "Russellian" approach (not to be confused with the Russellian hierarchy above). Their treatment is innovative in a number of respects, formally elegant throughout, and in large part serves to confirm the work above.

Both of Barwise and Etchemendy's models rely on Aczel set theory— ZFC/AFA, or Zermelo-Fraenkel set theory with an antifoundational axiom—as a basic tool for modeling certain classes of circular phenomena. In what follows, I simplify significantly in an attempt to avoid unnecessary technicalities. For my purposes, the important point regarding ZFC/AFA, for example, is simply that it includes sets that take themselves as members: Ω and α, for example, graphically representable as

Sets within ZFC/AFA are in fact individuated by their graphs: structurally identical sets are in all cases identical.[51]

Barwise and Etchemendy's two approaches also share a simple formal language L, though one that does include a unary (1-ary) relation **True**. The basic resources of L consist of the following.

Constant symbols: **Claire**, **Max**, and card symbols **2♣**, **3♣**, ..., **K♠**, **A♠**.

Propositional demonstratives: **this, that**$_1$, **that**$_2$, ...

Binary relation symbols: **Has, Believes**

A unary relation symbol: **True**

Logical connectives: &, ∨, ∼.[52]

Such a language thus contains a stock of sentences regarding Claire, Max, and the having of particular cards: **(Max Has 3♣)** and **(Max Has 3♣)** ∨ **(Claire Has 3♣)**, for example. But it also contains sentences that look like the Liar: ∼ **True(this)**.

What Barwise and Etchemendy's Russellian and Austinian approaches technically provide are rival semantics for such a formal language. Here we will also be concerned, as are Barwise and Etchemendy themselves, with the possibility of extending such approaches to far richer languages as well.

The Russellian approach

On both approaches, propositions are modeled as set-theoretic objects within ZFC/AFA. Within the Russellian approach, for example, the proposition that Claire has the ace of clubs is modeled as an ordered quintuple ⟨*Prop*, Having, Claire, A♣, 1⟩, the proposition that she does not as ⟨*Prop*, Having, Claire, A♣, 0⟩. For brevity I represent these as [Claire *H* A♣] and $\overline{[\text{Claire } H \text{ A♣}]}$.[53] Propositions are now assigned to sentences in fairly predictable ways: the sentence **(Max Has 3♣)** is assigned the proposition [Max *H* 3♣], for example, and the sentence **(Max Has 3♣)** ∨ **(Claire Has 3♣)** the proposition [Max *H* 3♣] ∨ [Claire *H* 3♣].

Most important for our purposes, perhaps, is the fact that the Liar sentence (λ) ∼ **True(this)**, far from being taken to express *no* proposition, is taken to express the unique circular proposition $f = \overline{[Tr f]}$.

States of affairs are introduced as set-theoretic objects of the form ⟨*H, a, c; i*⟩, ⟨*Tr, p; i*⟩ or ⟨*Bel, a, p; i*⟩, where *a* is Claire or Max, *c* is a card, *p* a proposition, and *i* is 1 or 0 as an obtaining or not obtaining indicator, respectively. A situation is simply a subset of the class of states of affairs. The notion of a situation *s* making a proposition *p* true, $s \models p$, is now fairly straightforward. In part,

$s \models [a H c]$ iff ⟨*H, a, c; 1*⟩ ∈ *s*,

$s \models [Tr p]$ iff ⟨*Tr, p; 1*⟩ ∈ *s*.

To depict the role played by the world in determining the facts and hence the truth of propositions, Barwise and Etchemendy introduce the notion of a model of the world. Within the Russellian account, models of the world are maximal weak models that are almost semantically closed: M qualifies as a model of the world just in case M is a collection of states of affairs (soa's) such that

1. no soa and its dual are in M (M is coherent);

2. $\langle Tr, p; 1 \rangle \in M$ iff $M \models p$, and $\langle Tr, p; 0 \rangle \in M$ iff $M \models \bar{p}$ (M is almost semantically closed);

3. M is not properly contained in any other set of soa's satisfying (1) and (2) (M is maximal).

Here it should be noted that the second part of condition (2) is not, and is importantly distinct from, a requirement that $\langle Tr, p; 0 \rangle \in M$ iff $M \not\models p$. This stronger requirement would give us a semantically closed model and, for any language with the resources of L, inconsistency as well.

   Within the Russellian model, then, we have ZFC/AFA set-theoretic objects as models for propositions and situations. We are given a semantics that assigns propositions to the sentences of L and that offers truth conditions for propositions in terms of states of affairs contained in models of the world.

   With respect to the Liar, the upshot is this. We can speak of a proposition as made true by a model M if $M \models p$, and as made false by M if $M \not\models p$. By contrast, let us speak of a proposition as *true in M* just in case $\langle Tr, p; 1 \rangle \in M$, and as *false in M* just in case $\langle Tr, p; 0 \rangle \in M$. In these terms it becomes clear that the Liar proposition f will be made false by every model M. The alternative would be $M \models f$, which would give us contradiction. Nonetheless, it is also clear that the Liar will be false in *no* model M.

   Barwise and Etchemendy are quite forthright about the lesson of incompleteness that this carries regarding the world as a whole:

Intuitively,...once we see that the Liar really *isn't* true, it seems that this fact should itself be a genuine feature of the world, a feature capable of influencing the truth or falsity of propositions. But of course it cannot be. For if it were, this would in turn make the Liar true, just as the intuitive reasoning predicts, and we would then have a contradiction, a violation of an even more closely held intuition....

What are we to make of this odd consequence of the Russellian account? If we take it seriously, it does indeed yield a diagnosis of the paradox, but a rather unsettling one. From this perspective, where our intuitive reasoning goes wrong is in thinking the world encompasses everything that is the case. (1987, 105)

The apparent lessons of the Russellian approach, then, seem to be precisely the lessons I have stressed throughout.[54] In Barwise and Etchemendy's terms, "What we give up on the Russellian view is the totality of the world" (174).

The Austinian model

Barwise and Etchemendy also offer a second account, which may at first sight seem to avoid such a conclusion. On the Austinian approach, they claim, though we salvage virtually all our pretheoretic intuitions about truth and falsity, "both the coherence and the totality of the world is preserved" (1987, 173).

Here, as in the Russellian case, they offer a formal semantics for the simple language L, and here as there set-theoretic objects from Aczel set theory are used to model both propositions and situations. In the Austinian case, however, all propositions are taken to be of the form $\{s; T\}$, where s is a situation and T a situation type: all propositions are explicitly or implicitly to the effect that a particular situation—what the proposition is about—is of a particular type.

Classes of states of affairs, situations, types and propositions are co-defined as follows, where the closure Γ of X is the smallest collection containing X and closed under (infinite) disjunction and conjunction and the class $TYPE$ of all types is $\Gamma(AtTYPE)$.

Let SOA, SIT, $AtTYPE$, and $PROP$ be the largest classes satisfying the following conditions:[55]

- Every $\sigma \in SOA$ is of the form $\langle H, a, c; i \rangle$, $\langle Tr, p; i \rangle$, or $\langle Bel, a, p; i \rangle$.
- Every $s \in SIT$ is a subset of SOA.
- Every $p \in PROP$ is of the form $\{s; T\}$, where $s \in SIT$ and $T \in \Gamma(AtTYPE)$.
- Every $T \in AtTYPE$ is of the form $[\sigma]$, where $\sigma \in SOA$.

A situation s is of a simple type $[\sigma]$ just in case $\sigma \in s$, and it is of disjunctive types $[\bigwedge X]$ or $[\bigvee X]$ just in case it's of all types $T \in X$ or some types $T \in X$ respectively.[56] A proposition $\{s, T\}$ is said to be *true* just in case s is of type T.

At this point there are already a number of strange features of such an account that should be noted. Truth and falsity as Barwise and Etchemendy portray them have essentially nothing to do with the way the world happens to be. Whether a proposition is true or not depends only on whether the contents of its type—σ in the simple case of $[\sigma]$, for example—are elements of the situation s that it is about. Since situations are simply sets of abstract states of affairs, all propositions retain their truth values no matter how the world happens to be. Truth, on such a view, seems to have come unstuck from the contingency of the world.

Given some straightforward additions to the basic language, then, an entirely fictional scene portrayed by Conan Doyle would qualify as a set of states of affairs and hence as a situation. Propositions about that situation and to the effect that Holmes is smoking a Meerschaum, received a letter from a penitent Vicar, or even is a real person would be simply *true*. But things become even more curious. For among sets of states of affairs, and hence situations, will be "contradictory" situations such as that in which I am both taller than the Empire State Building and shorter or that in which it's both true and false that $2 + 2 = 4$. A proposition about a situation of the first sort and to the effect that I am taller than the Empire State Building will be simply true; indeed, a proposition about such a situation and to the effect that I am both taller than the Empire State Building *and* am *not* will simply be *true*.

On such a view, *all* propositions are simply propositions about (abstract) situations and to the effect that those situations belong to certain situation types, essentially to the effect that the σ of situation type $[\sigma]$ is a member of the situation in question. What we might standardly take as a contingent proposition, then, such as the claim that Gary is sick today, can at best be a proposition to the effect that the situation s referred to is of a type in which Gary is sick today. On the plausible assumption that situations are to be individuated on the basis of what holds in them, however, all such propositions appear to be *necessary* claims, set-theoretic claims, in fact, regarding merely the contents of particular abstract situations. The upshot is that although a proposition to the effect that Gary is sick today may be true of a particular situation, that does not yet tell us whether the situation in question is one we confront in the contingent world as we know it. Knowledge that such a proposition is *true*, in fact, would be insufficient to tell us whether Gary happens to be sick today.[57]

These oddities regarding the notions of propositions and situations as they appear in such an account should at least serve as a warning that these terms, as technically defined, may not carry their standard metaphysical significance. The "situations," "propositions," and "world" of Barwise and

Etchemendy's model may not in the end genuinely fill the philosophical
roles that their titles suggest.

Although the world does not enter the Austinian picture in determining
truth and falsity, it does enter it in another way. On the Austinian account,
a total model U of the world is a collection of states of affairs such that the
following hold:

1. No soa and its dual are in U. If $\langle Tr, p; 1 \rangle \in U$, then p is true. If
$\langle Tr, p; 0 \rangle \in U$, then p is false.

2. U is not properly contained in other classes of soa's satisfying (1).

Situation s is *actual* in a model if $s \subseteq U$, and a proposition is said to be
accessible if the situation it is about is actual in U. Now although there
are propositions, even true propositions, about nonexistent and for that
matter impossible situations, only those about "actual" situations are said
to be "accessible" or "expressible."

In slightly greater detail, though I still simplify significantly, propositions are assigned within the Austinian account not to sentences per se but
to "statements" Φ, taken as pairs of sentences ϕ and contexts c_s. A *legitimate* statement is one such that situation s of context c_s is actual. The
proposition $Exp(\Phi)$ said to be expressed by a statement Φ is now assigned
very much in the manner of the Russellian account, though here the assignment is somewhat complicated by the addition of situations. Sentences of
the form **(a Has c)**, for example, are assigned propositions $\{s; [H, a, c; 1]\}$.
Where Φ is a "legitimate" statement, $Exp(\Phi)$ will in all cases be an "accessible" proposition.

Here as before it is crucially important to keep certain formal features
of Barwise and Etchemendy's model distinct from the philosophical terminology used to label those features. The formalism alone, for example, in
no way indicates that what is termed "accessibility" has anything to do
with what propositions we can actually entertain or what propositions our
knowledge can give us access to. On the basis of the formal model alone,
the "expressibility" of propositions need have nothing to do with what our
language allows us to express. Those propositions "accessible" relative to
a model U, after all, are simply those propositions about situations set-
theoretically included in the model. Any claim that given the situations of
an actual world U, one could have no epistemic or linguistic access to
propositions about *other* situations would require philosophical argument
far beyond anything a formal model alone could supply.

That warning aside, however, what happens to the Liar within the Austinian approach? Here, as in the Russellian case, there *will* be genuine Liar propositions. For any situation s, in fact, there will be a circular proposition $f_s = \{s; [Tr, f_s; 0]\}$ to the effect that the falsity of f_s is a fact about s.

Given any *actual* situation in any model, however, the Liar proposition f_s about that situation will be false. It follows that any Liar proposition accessible in any model of the world will be false. Here the contrary assumption simply leads to contradiction. If f_s is true, then $\langle Tr, f_s; 0 \rangle \in s$. Since s is actual in some model U, however, f_s must then be false, by the definition of 'model of the world'.

What of the falsity of the Liar for a situation s? That fact cannot be included in the situation s in question for the same reason that the falsity of the Liar within a Russellian maximal model can't be included in that model. In each case we would face contradiction. Each situation on the Austinian account thus faces precisely the limitations of "the world" on the Russellian account: its Liar proposition, though made false *by* the situation, cannot be false *in* it.

How, then, can Barwise and Etchemendy claim to have preserved "virtually all our pretheoretic intuitions" (1987, 164), in particular, with regard to the totality of the world? On the Austinian account, the falsity of the Liar about some situation s, though it cannot be included in s, *can* be included in the maximal model of the world U.

Within such an account, Barwise and Etchemendy concede, there does remain an essential partiality: "The partiality is not a property of the world itself, but of those parts of the world that propositions can be about. Or if we think of it in terms of language, we see that while the world is as total as one could want, we cannot, in general, make statements about the world as a whole" (1987, 154).

Within the Austinian account, in fact, the world as a whole simply does not and cannot qualify as a situation, as one of those things a proposition might be about. Some situations, of course, are nonactual. But that does not apply to the world. Within the Austinian account as it stands, the world is not a situation at all, either actual or nonactual.

This conclusion, implicit in much of the Austinian development, can be made explicit and removed from our particular model of propositions. Assume that there are propositions of the sort modeled in this part of the book, and that they are about portions of the real world, portions we will call 'actual situations'. We begin with the general observation that facts about certain propositions automatically diagonalize out of the actual situations those propositions are about. Thus for any actual situation s, the falsehood of its Liar f_s simply cannot be a fact of s. This is analogous to the general observation that for any set a (wellfounded or not), the Russell set $z_a = \{x \in a \mid x \notin x\}$ cannot be a member of a. From either of these observations we may draw a more specific conclusion. From the latter, we can conclude that no set is universal, that no set contains all sets as members: any candidate for the universal set u will at least omit the set z_u, and hence fail to be universal. Just so, from the former observation we can conclude that no actual situation is universal, that no actual situation can contain all the facts of the world. For no matter how comprehensive we take an actual situation w to be, it must at least omit the first-class fact that f_w is false. Thus, just as the Russell construction shows that there cannot be a universal set, the Liar construction shows that the situations propositions can be about fall short of universality. (1987, 155)

The technical manifestation of the fact that the world does not qualify as a situation is that it is itself a class rather than a set of states of affairs. Nonetheless, the essential reason why such an approach cannot countenance the world as a situational whole goes deeper:

The diagonal argument given above shows that something like the set/class distinction is forced on us in modeling the Austinian conception. To be sure, we could have guaranteed that total models were sets by restricting both situations and propositions to be smaller than some fixed cardinality. But then the Liar construction would show that our models of the world, though sets, are too big to be situations. Thus it is unavoidable that Austinian models of the world outstrip their constituent situations, if not due to the set/class distinction, then for other reasons. (155)[58]

To the Russellian conclusion that there can be no maximal or complete world, then, corresponds the Austinian conclusion that there can be no maximal or complete *situation*, no situation that includes all facts or all actual states of affairs. In one sense, then, Barwise and Etchemendy have preserved a total "world" at the cost of abandoning it as situational. What are actual are situations; the world, since it's not a situation, cannot be actual in that sense.

Another way of making the point, perhaps more pointedly, is this. Since the world is not a situation, on such an approach there are not merely no "expressible" or "accessible" propositions about the world but no propositions about the world at all. Though we are assured that there *is* a complete world, then, there is no true proposition about that world and to the effect that it is complete, or even to the effect that it exists at all.

Here it's clear that a number of basic philosophical notions have come unglued in the course of formal modeling, however elegant that modeling may be in other respects. For a quite fundamental intuitive principle is that for each thing there is and each property it has, there are both (1) a state of affairs, the state of affairs of its having that property, and (2) a proposition to the effect that it has that property. Within the Austinian account, however, terminology has shifted in such a way as to violate such basic intuitions. Although we are told that there *is* an actual world, and though there are presumably things true of it—or at least properties of it to which Barwise and Etchemendy's theory commits them—there simply are no true propositions about it and to the effect that it has those properties. For there are no propositions about it at all.[59]

Consider also a problem related to difficulties raised earlier regarding propositional accounts. Though Barwise and Etchemendy explicitly confine themselves to a quite limited formal language, they envisage richer extensions as well, and in particular extensions richer in semantic terminology. Within such an extension, still in the spirit of their account, consider the following:

'Appended to its own quotation can be used to express no true proposition about the entire world' appended to its own quotation can be used to express no true proposition about the entire world.

Were such a sentence capable of expressing a true proposition about the entire world, of course, it would not be. Any proposition it expressed regarding the entire world would then necessarily be false. On Barwise and Etchemendy's Austinian account, we've noted, *no* sentence can be used to express any proposition about the entire world. But what holds for all sentences will hold for this one, and clearly what can express no proposition can express no true proposition. Barwise and Etchemendy would thus seem committed to the claim that

'Appended to its own quotation can be used to express no true proposition about the entire world' appended to its own quotation can be used to express no true proposition about the entire world.

So have Barwise and Etchemendy preserved a total "world"? Only at the cost of violating the basic principle that for everything that is the case (or for that matter, that is not), there is a proposition to the effect that it is the case. On that ground alone it seems dubious whether the "propositions" their model countenances can be considered propositions in the full and familiar philosophical sense. It's also clear, however, that such a sacrifice is fundamental to the basic strategy of the account. Were we to attempt to alter it so as to do justice to that fundamental intuition, all earlier conclusions would stand in full generality. For any collection of true propositions, there would be some proposition it excluded. Any "world" corresponding to a collection of true propositions would necessarily be incomplete.[60]

Barwise and Etchemendy's innovative work has enriched the literature on the Liar enormously, not only by the introduction of a number of powerful tools for set-theoretic modeling but by the clear portrayal of a fresh and welcome approach to modeling itself. But any claim that they have solved the Liar or have saved a complete and consistent world is far too strong.

10   Conclusion

In opening sections I began with Liar-like arguments against a set of all truths, against a common approach to possible worlds, and against a notion of omniscience. The *apparent* lesson of such arguments is that all of these notions must be abandoned as incoherent.

We have also considered a broad range of possible responses: appeals to truth-value gaps and truth-value gluts, to many-valued logics and propositions, to a range of hierarchial treatments and the complexities of Barwise and Etchemendy's Austinian model. With the exception of approaches that in one way or another involve an appeal to hierarchy, however, *none* of these seems genuinely adequate against either the Liar or Liar-like arguments.

In the end, an appeal to hierarchy of one sort or another seems to emerge as the strongest candidate for an adequate treatment of the Liar. Such an approach, however, far from saving a totality of truths, set-theoretic worlds, or omniscience, *itself* excludes these as incoherent.

Is the notion of a totality of truth, or of total knowledge, then *in fact* incoherent? So the argument as a whole seems to suggest. It must nonetheless be admitted that the argument is only as strong as an unanswered challenge. One may be perfectly justified in wondering whether some new response, or some variation on an old one, may yet offer a way out.

Far too often, however, it is asked what has gone wrong with paradox rather than what paradox may have to teach us. What the Liar may genuinely have to teach us, I think, is that there really can be no coherent notion of all truth or of omniscience. The argument becomes stronger, moreover, as it becomes clear that a broad class of logical results suggest very much the same conclusion.

Such is the course of the following chapters.

2 Truth, Omniscience, and the Paradox of the Knower

In "A Paradox Regained" David Kaplan and Richard Montague offer a purified form of the paradox of the surprise examination that they call the paradox of the Knower.[1] In later work, Montague uses a form of the paradox against syntactical treatments of modality.[2]

The full impact of the Knower, however, has not yet been realized—or so I will argue. For what the Knower offers is a surprisingly powerful argument against the coherence of a broad range of common notions if taken in full generality. Most important for my purposes here, it offers an intriguing argument against any notion of a totality of truth or of total knowledge.[3]

In the first three sections that follow, I want to outline the paradox and sketch what I take to be its general impact, with truth and omniscience foremost in mind. Here, as in the case of the Liar, a number of responses are possible, of course. In sections 4 through 7, I consider possible ways out.

1 The Paradox of the Knower

The paradox of the Knower is a somewhat complex but solid argument for the surprising conclusion that an apparently innocuous list of statements is in fact inconsistent.

Let us start by borrowing the syntax (alphabet and grammar) of any system adequate for arithmetic. Here, for example, we can use system Q of Robinson arithmetic. To the alphabet of such a system let us add the single symbol '$\triangle$'. We broaden the grammar so as to include '$\triangle(x)$' as a well-formed formula (where numerals will fill in for 'x'), and specify that '$\triangle(x)$' will form compound wffs in the standard ways.

So far, then, we have simply broadened slightly the acceptably grammatical class of wffs. All standard symbols will retain their standard interpretations, and '$\triangle$' can for the present be thought of as some sort of knowledge predicate. More about '$\triangle$' in a moment.

The language of the list of statements at issue can be borrowed in this way from any system adequate for arithmetic. The first statements in the list are borrowed from the same source and consist simply of the axioms of the system at issue. To use system Q as an example, then, the first entries on the list will be these:[4]

$$\forall x \forall y (Sx = Sy \rightarrow x = y)$$

$$\forall x (0 \neq Sx)$$

$$\forall x [x \neq 0 \rightarrow \exists y (x = Sy)]$$

$$\forall x [(x + 0) = x]$$

$$\forall x \forall y [(x + Sy) = S(x + y)]$$

$$\forall x [(x \cdot 0) = 0]$$

$$\forall x \forall y [(x \cdot Sy) = (x \cdot y) + x].$$

On the standard interpretation we take all of these to be true, of course, both because they seem transparently true (in the vernacular, the second amounts to, 'Zero is the successor of no natural number', for example) and because we take *arithmetic* to be true.

Note now two key facts. The first is this. All strings of symbols within the language we are using, including those in which '$\triangle$' appears, can be recoverably encoded as numbers. This is guaranteed simply by the fact that the strings of any such language can be so encoded. To such numbers there will in turn correspond numerals within the language of the system at issue. Assuming a particular Gödel numbering, then, let us refer to the numeral that corresponds to a string A as $\bar{A}$. '$\triangle(\bar{A})$' will be the application of '$\triangle$' to a numeral $\bar{A}$ corresponding to that Gödel number encoding formula A. Quite generally, given an assumed encoding, I will refer to $\bar{A}$ as the Gödel *numeral* of A.

The second key fact is this. What we have implicitly outlined so far is a *system* Q', consisting of the syntax of Q broadened to include '$\triangle$' and the axioms of Q, borrowed for the list. Within system Q' some formulas will, of course, be derivable from others: formula B with Gödel numeral $\bar{B}$ will be derivable from formula A with Gödel numeral $\bar{A}$, perhaps. In Q', as in Q and any other system adequate for arithmetic, we will be able to define a derivability relation $I(x, y)$ such that for any A and B, if B is derivable from A then $\vdash I(\bar{A}, \bar{B})$.

We now have notation in hand to complete the list at issue. I have proposed that '$\triangle$' is to be read as a knowledge predicate of some kind, but I have been anything but specific about that and will in fact entertain a broad range of interpretations in what follows. For now, let us use '$\triangle(\bar{A})$' to mean 'the formula with Gödel numeral $\bar{A}$ is known to be true', or simply 'formula A is known to be true'.[5] And let us add to the list claims indicated by the following schemata:

$$\triangle(\bar{A}) \rightarrow A \tag{1}$$

$$\triangle(\overline{\triangle(\bar{A}) \rightarrow A}) \tag{2}$$

$$I(\bar{A}, \bar{B}) \rightarrow. \ \triangle(\bar{A}) \rightarrow \triangle(\bar{B}) \tag{3}$$

On the outlined interpretation, these will read, in effect, as follows

If something is known to be so, it is so. (4)

(4) is known to be so. (5)

If B is derivable from A in Q', then if A is known to be so,
B is known to be so.[6] (6)

We can express the paradox of the Knower as follows. The constructed list, composed merely of axioms borrowed from Q and the claims indicated in the three schemata above, is provably inconsistent. If the initial axiomatic items of the list are true, the auxiliary claims concerning knowledge logically *cannot* be true.

This will hold, moreover, for whatever interpretation we choose to give for '$\triangle$'. For no notion of knowledge—or anything else, for that matter—can claims represented by the three schemata above be true.

2   The Argument

The technical argument for this paradoxical conclusion builds on the diagonal lemma, provable for Q':

DIAGONAL LEMMA   For any formula $B(y)$ of Q' containing just the variable y free, there is a sentence G of Q' such that $G \equiv B(\bar{G})$ is demonstrable as a theorem.[7]

Let us use '$\triangle(neg(y))$' in place of $B(y)$, where 'neg' is a recursive function representable in Q' that gives us the Gödel numeral of the negation of the formula with Gödel numeral y. Then by the diagonal lemma, there will in particular be a sentence S of Q' such that

$$\vdash S \equiv \triangle(neg(S))$$

or simply

$\vdash S \equiv \triangle(\overline{\sim S}).^8$

Note that for '$\vdash$' or 'provable in Q'' here we might also substitute 'derivable from the initial entries of the list', since these are simply the axioms of Q'.

Now let us take that instance of schema (1) in which '$\sim S$' appears in place of 'A'. I will call this instance (7):

$$\triangle(\overline{\sim S}) \to \sim S \tag{7}$$

Now (7) together with $\vdash S \equiv \triangle(\overline{\sim S})$ gives us

$S \to \sim S.$

So

$(7) \vdash S \to \sim S.$

But then, of course,

$(7) \vdash \sim S.$

That is, $\sim S$ is derivable from (7), an instance of schema (1).

If a derivability relation of this sort holds, as noted, this will itself be demonstrable in Q' in the form

$\vdash I((\overline{7}), \overline{\sim S}).$

Schema (2), of course, gives us

$$\triangle((\overline{7})). \tag{8}$$

Consider now schema (3) with '$(\overline{7})$' and '$\overline{\sim S}$' in place of '$\overline{A}$' and '$\overline{B}$'. This gives us

$$\triangle((\overline{7})) \to \triangle(\overline{\sim S}). \tag{9}$$

By modus ponens,

$(8), (9) \vdash \triangle(\overline{\sim S}).$

Using the derivable fact that $S \equiv \triangle(\overline{\sim S})$, we then get

$(8), (9) \vdash S.$

From the steps above, we now have $(8), (9) \vdash S$ and $(7) \vdash \sim S$. Thus,

$(7), (8), (9) \vdash S \ \& \sim S.$

But, of course, (7), (8), and (9) are merely particular instances of schemata (1) through (3). Given what can be derived from the initial axiomatic entries of the list, then, the three auxiliary schemata lead to contradiction. The list as a whole, however plausible its entries individually and whatever interpretation we choose for '△', is inconsistent.

3 The Power of the Paradox

What the argument above really shows is that for no '△' can all three of schemata (1) through (3) be consistently maintained. Or at least, for no '△' can these three be maintained consistently with the axioms of any system adequate for arithmetic. Arithmetic, surely, is not to be abandoned.

This is, I think, a very powerful result precisely because there are many common and important notions for which we *would* intuitively insist on all three schemata above. What the argument shows is that we can't.

In what follows, I want to outline implications of the Knower, or at least apparent implications, for notions of knowledge and truth. But this is merely a first sketch. Whether the apparent implications of the Knower are genuine or merely apparent is a matter that requires careful consideration of possible replies in subsequent sections.

With only the interpretation sketched for '△' so far in mind, however, the argument above might not appear to have a particularly startling result. For let us take '△' as 'is known by ____', where we fill in the blank with the name of a particular person; let us take '△' as 'is known by Patrick Grim', for example.

Here schema (1) $(\triangle(\bar{A}) \to A)$ will apparently hold simply because knowledge, in order to be knowledge, must be veridical. Schema (2) might hold if Grim knows this. But (3),

$$I(\bar{A}, \bar{B}) \to . \triangle(\bar{A}) \to \triangle(\bar{B}),$$

seems quite *unlikely* to hold for Grim or any comparable agent; Grim surely does *not* know every logical consequence of the things he knows. If (3) is false on the face of it, an argument that (1) through (3) cannot all be true may not seem particularly unsettling.

Within a system of epistemic logic such as that offered by Hintikka in *Knowledge and Belief* (1967) something like (3) *will* hold.[9] For given any $p \to q$ valid in ordinary propositional logic, one is committed in such a system to

$Kap \rightarrow Kaq,$

with 'Kap' read as 'a knows that p'.[10]

Precisely this principle, however, has been widely thought to be a particularly implausible feature of such systems.[11] Here again, if (3) is implausible on its own, the fact that (1) through (3) cannot be true together might seem a less than startling result.

Even here, however, the argument for the Knower should give us pause. For although Grim does not know all consequences of what he knows, this would intuitively seem to be a contingent limitation; it just so happens that he is not an ideal knower. Hintikka's original defense of something like schema (3) in his account is similarly to stress its idealistic intent: "Our results are not directly applicable to what is true or false in the actual world of ours. They tell us something definite only in a world in which everybody follows the consequences of what he knows as far as they lead him."[12]

What the argument above shows, however, is not merely that the three schemata are not *in fact* true together. What it shows is that they logically *cannot* be true together.

That (1) through (3) do not hold, where '△' is read as 'is known by Grim' thus appears not to be merely a contingent limitation of Grim. That the knowers that we know do not satisfy (1) through (3) is apparently not to be shrugged off by appeal to ideal knowers. For what the argument seems to show is that such ideal knowers are as logically impossible as married bachelors or circular squares. The ideal itself appears to be incoherent.

We can perhaps make the point clearer, and the impact of the paradox more forceful, if we interpret '△' not as 'is known by Grim' or the like but as 'is in principle knowable'. Now all of the schemata would seem to hold, regardless of our personal or present limitations, given an optimistic enough view of the extendibility of knowledge in principle. If 'knowable in principle' is taken to include 'knowable on the basis of (unlimited) demonstration within Q'', the truth of our troublesome schema (3) would in fact seem to be guaranteed.

The argument of the Knower will hold, however, regardless of what interpretation we choose for '△'. Thus it appears that not even for knowability in principle can our three schemata hold, no matter how far we choose to stretch 'in principle'. Alternatively put, any knowledge in principle for which (1) through (3) *would* hold appears to be logically impossible.

Let us read '△', finally, as 'is known by an omniscient God'. Surely now all of our schemata must be true. For they read, in effect, as follows:

If something is known by an omniscient God, it is so.   (10)

(10) is known by an omniscient God.   (11)

If B is derivable from A and A is known by an omniscient God,
then B is known by an omniscient God.   (12)

The force of the argument, however, is that these logically cannot all be true. Genuine omniscience would demand no less, and thus it appears that there logically cannot be any omniscient being.

Up to this point I have emphasized the implications of the paradox for notions of knowledge. But the argument at issue will hold for any interpretation of '△', epistemic or not, and thus the paradox of the Knower will apply to other common notions as well.[13]

One of these is truth—not surprising, perhaps, in virtue of certain points of contact between Montague's original development of the Knower and Tarski's theorem. If '△' is read simply as 'is true', all three schemata would seem patently obvious:

If something is true, it is so.   (13)

(13) is true.   (14)

If B follows from A and A is true, then B is true as well.   (15)

But no more for '△' as truth than for '△' as knowledge will these be consistent with axioms for arithmetic. Even a notion of *truth* for which (1) through (3) would hold, it appears, must prove incoherent.[14]

Consider, finally, possible worlds outlined as in chapter one: possible worlds construed in terms of maximal consistent sets of propositions. Here using α to refer to that maximal set of truths corresponding to the actual world, let us read '△' as 'is a member of set α'. All schemata now seem beyond reproach:

If something is a member of α, it obtains (or is the case).[15]   (16)

(16) is a member of α.   (17)

If B follows from A and A is a member of α, then B is a member of
α as well.   (18)

But here again it appears that these cannot be consistent with axioms for arithmetic. In the case of the Knower, as in the case of the Liar, set-theoretic possible worlds seem to fall victim as well.

But does the argument above genuinely have these philosophical implications, or are they merely apparent? Formal arguments and their philosophical implications are subtle things, and here, as before, we must carefully consider possible replies.

4 Possible Ways Out

What the argument of section 2 shows is that for no '△' can all three of the schemata above consistently be maintained. This much, moreover, is a solidly formal result. We may be able to philosophize around it, but we won't be able to philosophize it away.

As noted in the preceding section, however, (1) through (3) do intuitively seem to hold for a range of common notions, including common notions of truth and knowledge—at least for knowability in principle and omniscience. Yet any notion of truth or knowledge for which these do hold must be abandoned as incoherent.

What are the possible ways out? The basic strategy of any escape here is to fight initial intuitions: to deny, despite appearances, that truth or knowledge in the sense at issue is something for which (1) through (3) will hold. Truth and knowledge are *not*, on such a strategy, properly represented by '△' in the schemata above.

In the sections that follow I want to consider several variations on this central strategy. Note that in the schemata above, '△' appears as a predicate, a single predicate and a predicate that applies to '$\overline{A}$' and the like as in effect names of sentences. One way out is to insist that although truth and knowledge do apply as predicates, they apply as predicates not of sentences but of something else—propositions perhaps. Another possible escape is to insist that 'is true' and 'is known' are not to be construed as predicates at all but as sentential operators or in the manner of redundancy theories of truth. A third way out, the most traditional and in many ways the simplest, is to concede truth and knowledge as predicates, and as predicates of sentences, but to deny that these can be represented by a *single* predicate, such as '△'. This is the strategy of the hierarchical reply. Each of these strategies of escape has something to be said for it, I think.[16] But none, I want to suggest, effectively obviates the force of the Knower with respect to a notion of all truth or of omniscience.

5   Propositions and the Strengthened Knower

Within the schemata of the Knower, '$\triangle$' appears as a predicate of sentences. One possible way out is to insist that knowledge and truth, so tempting and yet so disastrous as interpretations for '$\triangle$', are properties of something else instead. Here the traditional candidate is, of course, propositions.

As noted in chapter one, a major challenge for any propositional approach remains the construction of a coherent account that nonetheless does justice to the full range of informal intuitions. Here, however, I want to press a tidier objection against any propositional reply to the Knower. It won't work. In particular, any propositional reply will fall afoul of what C. Anthony Anderson terms the *Strengthened* Knower.[17]

Here it proves fruitful to distinguish a negative aspect from a positive aspect of the propositional response. The negative aspect is simply the charge that knowledge and truth cannot properly be represented by the '$\triangle$' of the three schemata. But that aspect alone, of course, fails to distinguish a propositional response from any other; it is simply the basic strategy of any response to the Knower.

What genuinely distinguishes the propositional response is its positive aspect. For what the propositionalist appears to have in mind is an alternative way of representing truth and knowledge. The *positive* propositional claim is that truth and knowledge apply not to sentences, as '$\triangle$' essentially does, but to some sort of propositions somehow *expressed* by sentences. It is this positive aspect of the propositional reply that falls afoul of the Strengthened Knower.

Suppose that we add to our language those symbols necessary to *properly* represent knowledge or truth as the propositionalist conceives them. Here we will need not only '$\triangle$', interpreted now as the *real* truth or knowledge predicate, but a mechanism for applying it strictly to propositions. Let us thus introduce '$E(\bar{A}, p)$' as an expression relation between sentences and propositions of precisely the type that the propositionalist proposes, where 'p' serves as a variable for propositions.[18] '$E(\bar{A}, p)$' then applies just in case the sentence with Gödel numeral $\bar{A}$ expresses proposition p.

Now, it appears, we will have the linguistic resources necessary for expressing genuine truth and knowledge predicates as the propositionalist conceives them. Note also that we need go no further in specifying what propositions *are*.[19]

Within such a language, however, the paradox reappears. For let us define '$\triangle$' as

$$\triangle(\bar{A}) =_{df} \exists p(E(\bar{A}, p) \ \& \ \triangle p),$$

in which '$\triangle$' applies—precisely as the propositionalist demands—to propositions alone.

Analogues of the previous schemata using $\triangle$ will now be propositionally unobjectionable. For

$$\triangle(\bar{A}) \to A \tag{19}$$

$$\triangle(\overline{\triangle(\bar{A}) \to A}) \tag{20}$$

$$I(\bar{A}, \bar{B}) \to. \ \triangle(\bar{A}) \to \triangle(\bar{B}) \tag{21}$$

will now read, in effect;

If the sentence with numeral $\bar{A}$ expresses a $\triangle$ proposition
(a true proposition, say, or one known by God), then A. \tag{22}

(22) expresses a $\triangle$ proposition. \tag{23}

If a sentence with numeral $\bar{A}$ expresses a $\triangle$ proposition and a sentence with numeral $\bar{B}$ follows from the one with numeral $\bar{A}$, then the sentence with numeral $\bar{B}$ also expresses a $\triangle$ proposition.[20] \tag{24}

Within Q', we noted, $S \equiv \triangle(\overline{\sim S})$ was demonstrable on the basis of axioms borrowed from Q. Within a system consisting of our expanded language and the same axioms there will similarly be a sentence U such that the following will be demonstrable:

$$U \equiv \triangle(\overline{\sim U}). \tag{25}$$

But now we have all the pieces needed—the demonstrable (25) and schemata for '$\triangle$'—to repeat the argument precisely as before.

The schemata even for '$\triangle$', then, will be inconsistent with any axioms for arithmetic, and this despite the fact that the knowledge or truth predicate '$\triangle$' is now reserved exclusively for propositions. The propositional reply apparently fails.[21]

What might a propositionalist say here? A propositionalist might insist that something has gone wrong in extending the language to include the expression relation $E(\bar{A}, p)$. Just as it was claimed that '$\triangle(\bar{A})$' did not capture the genuine knowledge or truth predicate, perhaps it might be claimed that '$E(\bar{A}, p)$' somehow fails to capture the genuine expression relation.

But it appears that the argument can be repeated for *whatever* general relation is proposed here. It appears, then, that if the notion of a proposition as something expressed by a sentence can itself be expressed at all—and that they are expressed by sentences is one of the few relatively clear things that *can* be said about propositions—the propositional proposal will fall afoul of the Strengthened Knower. Hence the justice of C. Anthony Anderson's comment regarding a propositional treatment of the Knower: "If we take the suggestion as something that can itself be expressed, the difficulty reappears" (Anderson 1983, 347).[22]

There is also, perhaps, a general lesson here. As indicated in chapter one, propositional approaches have often been faulted for incompleteness: for failing to make explicit what the expression relation between sentences and propositions is supposed to be, for example, in a way that would tell us which sentences will fail to express propositions and why. But the work here suggest that this is perhaps more than a contingent limitation. For given any expressible relation proposed between sentences and propositions, we can construct, in terms of that relation itself, a strengthened paradox that the propositionalist seems powerless to handle.

There is, however, one further way that the propositionalist might make objection to the Strengthened Knower stick. A propositionalist might insist that the expression of propositions by sentences cannot properly or coherently be represented by a *single* relation $E(\bar{A}, p)$.

Expression, it might be proposed, must instead be represented using a hierarchy of expression relations E_0, E_1, E_2, …, with familiar restrictions. An expression relation $E_n(\bar{A}, p)$ of this hierarchy, one might insist, can apply only to sentences involving expression relations with lower subscripts.

Such a move would indeed stop the Strengthened Knower in its tracks. We could not for example then use schema (20), in which stacked '$\triangle$'s are defined in terms of expression relations, in the manner required for paradox.[23]

There is also much to be said for such a proposal in other regards. It has been suggested, for example, that a broad range of terms call for hierarchical treatment, including perhaps truth, necessity, knowledge, belief, and other propositional attitudes (see Stebbins 1980 and Burge 1984). If so, however, it would seem desirable to centrally localize the *source* of hierarchy in all these cases. Given a propositional account of truth, necessity, knowledge, belief, and the like, a fundamental hierarchy within the expression relation would seem a very promising candidate in this regard.

A propositional approach *can* escape the Strengthened Knower, then, by means of auxiliary recourse to hierarchy. But a propositional treatment tempered with hierarchy will also inherit the difficulties of a purely hierarchical response.

6   Redundancy Theories and Operators

In section 5, I considered treating truth and knowledge, unlike the '△' of our schemata, as predicates of something other than sentences—with generally negative results.

Another possible way out is to insist that these are not legitimately predicates at all; they are, perhaps, to be treated as sentential *operators* instead.[24] This is essentially the route of redundancy theories of truth, exemplified by brief comments in Ramsey and developed elegantly in Dorothy L. Grover's "prosentential" theory.[25] Let me begin by concentrating on redundancy theories per se, broadening my comments at a later stage to include operator responses to the Knower in general.

At least initially, redundancy theories seem intuitively implausible; truth seems normally to be treated within English syntax as a straightforward predicate. Nonetheless, the guiding idea of redundancy theories is that the phrase 'is true' can be eliminated from all contexts without semantic loss. 'It is true that *p*', Ramsey argues, means nothing more than '*p*'.

As a treatment of cases in which '*p*' is overtly displayed, at least, this has much to be said for it. For if truth is not a predicate at all, we can conveniently avoid philosophical thickets both as to what it is a predicate *of* (sentences? propositions?) and what the conditions of its application are (correspondence? coherence? etc.).

But what of ordinary uses of 'true' in which '*p*' is not displayed, such as (26)?

All that Joe says is true.   (26)

Here it should be remembered that omniscience and a notion of all truths are among the basic concepts at stake. If (26) can't be expressed within the confines of a redundancy theory, it's clear that these can't either.

As Ramsey notes and Grover develops in detail, however, the effect of a truth predicate in such cases can be achieved using propositional quantification. For example, (26) becomes

$$\forall p(\text{Joe says that } p \rightarrow p). \tag{27}$$

Difficulties *may* remain. As Herbert Heidelberger notes, "It is not clear whether Ramsey intended the last occurrence of 'p' to fall within or outside the scope of the universal quantifier; either way, however, the paraphrase is unsuccessful. If 'p' falls within the scope of the quantifier, then it is an isolated variable to which no predicate is adjoined."[26] The predicate we are tempted to add, of course, is 'is true'. But were that required, the redundancy theory would clearly fail in the general attempt to eliminate truth as a predicate.

Here again, however, I want to press a tidier objection: that once redundancy theories are equipped to simulate a truth predicate by means of propositional quantification, as outlined above, they face both a form of the Liar and a form of the Strengthened Knower.

Consider first the Liar, and let us introduce the operator '§', which forms a term from a sentence. The symbol '§' might naturally be read, for example, as 'the statement that ...'.

Let 'c' abbreviate 'the statement made by sentence (28)', where (28) is

$$\forall p(c = \S p . \rightarrow \sim p). \tag{28}$$

Now empirically,

$$c = \S \forall p(c = \S p . \rightarrow \sim p). \tag{29}$$

But this is all we need to derive a contradiction in the standard manner of the Liar.[27]

Elimination of a truth predicate alone in the manner of redundancy theories thus fails to avoid a quantificational Liar. It is similarly insufficient—as is mere recourse to operators—to avoid a form of the Strengthened Knower.

As outlined above, the Strengthened Knower turns on a defined '△':

$$\triangle(\bar{A}) =_{\text{df}} \exists p(E(\bar{A}, p) \,\&\, \triangle p)$$

Redundancy theories of truth seem explicitly to demand propositional quantification of the form used here, as will operator views in general if adequate to express, for example,

All that God knows is true.   (30)

But here let us simply substitute '$N(\bar{A},p)$' in place of '$E(\bar{A},p)$', using '$N(\bar{A},p)$' to indicate that $\bar{A}$ forms a singular term for sentence p. One natural reading for '$N(\bar{A},p)$', for example, would be '$\bar{A}$ is the Gödel numeral of formula p'.

Now let

$$\triangle(\bar{A}) =_{\text{df}} \exists p(N(\bar{A},p) \ \& \ \triangle p).$$

Just as '$\triangle$' applied only to propositions in the earlier form of the Strengthened Knower, '$\triangle$' can here be interpreted purely as an operator on p.

Alternatively, a term-forming operator '§' could be introduced as above, using

$$\triangle(\bar{A}) =_{\text{df}} \exists p((\S p = \bar{A}) \ \& \ \triangle p).^{28}$$

In either case, though '$\triangle$' can now appear purely as an operator, the paradox of the Knower will reappear for '$\triangle$'. Note also that the paradox will hold for various interpretations of '$\triangle$'. In particular, the schemata for '$\triangle$' will seem obvious not only for '$\triangle$' as the operator 'is true', as in classical redundancy theories, but for '$\triangle$' as 'is knowable in principle' or 'is known by an omniscient God'. Appeal to operators alone, then, will quite generally prove insufficient against the Knower.[29]

Yet there is an attractive way out here for redundancy theories and operator approaches in general: an auxiliary resort to hierarchy.

Both the Liar and the Knower as they appear above can effectively be blocked if term-forming operators and term-forming relations such as '§' and '$N(\bar{A},p)$' are made subject to a hierarchy or if propositional quantification itself is made subject to such a hierarchy. The first proposal is Gilbert Harman's (1971): that if 'p' is an expression of a language L, '§p' or the like can appear only in a metalanguage. The second proposal is what Grover favors in Grover 1973: that in a substitutional interpretation of quantification we allow as substitutions for 'p' only formulas with fewer quantifiers than that in which 'p' occurs.[30]

Resort to hierarchy of either sort will stop paradox precisely as before. In the case of the Strengthened Knower, for example, the stacked '$\triangle$'s of schema (20) are explicitly defined in terms of propositional quantification and a term-forming operator or term relation. Hierarchical restriction on either of these will thus prevent us from using $\triangle(\overline{\triangle(\overline{A})} \to A)$ in the manner required for paradox.

Pure redundancy and operator theories, without such an appeal to hierarchy, seem ultimately insufficient against the Knower. Any redundancy or operator theory modified by an auxiliary recourse to hierarchy, on the other hand, will predictably inherit the difficulties of a purely hierarchical response.

7 Hierarchy

The remaining hope for a response to the Knower, it seems, is recourse to hierarchy, either in a pure form or as an attractive auxiliary to appeals to propositions or operators that prove insufficient without it.

Whatever the virtues of a hierarchical response in general, however, it appears it will prohibit both any global notion of truth suitable for speaking of *all* truth and any coherent notion of total knowledge. If hierarchy is required to escape the contradictions of the Knower, then, abandonment of any notion of all truth or of omniscience seems a necessary cost of that escape.

The classical hierarchies of Russell, Tarski, and Kripke were considered in chapter one with an eye to the Liar, and with precisely this result. It is clear that their implications for the Knower will be the same: though any of these can effectively block that pattern of reasoning essential to the Knower, they can do so only at the cost of abandoning fully general notions of truth and knowledge.

Here I want to reemphasize this basic lesson, while slightly extending the previous treatment of hierarchy, by considering an intriguing indexical-schematic account offered by Tyler Burge.[31]

In Burge, as in Tarski, truth appears only with implicit subscripts, and paradox is avoided by similar restrictions on the application of subscripted truth predicates. Burge's approach, however, is to take truth as an indexical notion. 'True' is to remain constant in meaning; subscripts are to indicate its shifting extensions, fixed pragmatically by context.[32]

What is of most interest for my purposes is the following. Burge effectively admits that a purely indexical account would afford us no way of making sense of a global notion of truth, suitable for "All statements are either true or not" or "God is omniscient" (Burge 1979, 191). For precisely that reason, however, he ultimately insists on a dual, indexical-*schematic* account. Most uses of the predicate 'true' in natural language are indexical, Burge proposes, but some are schematic.[33] Global applications of 'true' are to be represented as schematic generalizations:

> The subscripts marking contexts of use stand open, ready to be filled in as the occasions arise.... The first sentence above ["All sentences are true or not"], for example, should be formalized: $\forall s(\mathrm{Tr}_i(s) \vee \sim \mathrm{Tr}_i(s))$. When we judge the schematic statement itself to be true, we make an equally schematic statement with the context of our evaluation schematically fixed at $\ulcorner \mathrm{true}_{i+1} \urcorner$. (Burge 1979, 192)

This crucial passage, however, is bewilderingly obscure. For what Burge offers us here in place of a statement concerning all statements, or a sentence concerning all sentences, is something that itself is not and cannot be a statement or a sentence at all. It is a bare and empty schema, essentially incomplete and by its very nature distinct from the category of sentences and statements—that category of things that genuinely *can* have truth values. Nonetheless, Burge immediately goes on to speak of judging the "schematic statement" itself to be true.

We *could* legitimately treat Burge's example of a global principle of bivalence as a genuine statement, of course, were we to treat it in terms of universal quantification over indexical subscripts. Schemata in fact *are* often interpreted as involving implicit quantification in a metalanguage, and it is far from clear how *else* to interpret them.[34] Nonetheless, Burge is quite clear that the subscripts of

$$\forall s(\mathrm{Tr}_i(s) \vee \sim \mathrm{Tr}_i(s)) \tag{31}$$

and the like are *not* to be understood in terms of quantification: "For quantification into the argument place will provide an open sentence just as subject to paradox as the 'naive' truth-predicate formalization.... For example, one might suggest a sentence like (a), '(a) is not true at any level'" (Burge 1979, 192). Burge thus seems to want sentences such as (31) to serve both as pure schemata of some sort not open to quantification over their subscripts and as "schematic *statements*" themselves either true or false. These may simply be inconsistent desiderata.

Here perhaps we can simplify the matter, however. Questions of quantification over subscripts aside and, for the sake of argument, allowing (31) to have a truth value, can we also take (31) to be genuinely global, as providing a principle of bivalence that governs, for example, its own truth as well?

Apparently not. For if genuinely global, (31) will in some way take itself as a substituend:

$$\text{Tr}_i(31) \vee \sim\text{Tr}_i(31)$$

But here we have implicitly stacked 'Tr_i's, in apparent violation of the hierarchical stricture that a truth predicate be applicable only to formulas involving truth predicates with lower indices.

A new schema, taking perhaps schemata as substituends, *will* give us a principle of bivalence adequate for (31):

$$\forall s(\text{Tr}_{i+1}(s) \vee \sim\text{Tr}_{i+1}(s)) \tag{32}$$

But (32) will again fail to be genuinely global, since it too will be unable to take itself as a substituend.

Moreover, if we attempt to make room for genuinely global statements by waiving hierarchical strictures against stacked predicates of the same level—at least in the special case of a 'Tr_i' used in "schematic statements," say—we get paradox again.

For consider

$$\sim\text{Tr}_i(33), \tag{33}$$

which we might term the Schematic Liar.

Of course, (33) is a schema. As such it is at least a "schematized direction for making statements," in Burge's terms, and in effect licenses the following list:

$$\sim\text{Tr}_1(33)$$

$$\sim\text{Tr}_2(33)$$

$$\sim\text{Tr}_3(33)$$

$$\vdots$$

But if (33) is also a schematic *statement*, what truth value can we assign to (33) itself?

To claim that (33) is true, after the passage quoted from Burge above, would be to claim that $\text{Tr}_{i+1}(33)$. But if we take '$i + 1$' at face value, this appears to be simply a further schema, a schema that licenses the following:

$Tr_2(33)$

$Tr_3(33)$

$Tr_4(33)$

$\vdots$

To claim that (33) is not true, on the other hand, would, on Burge's outline, be to claim that $\sim Tr_{i+1}(33)$. What this gives us is

$\sim Tr_2(33)$

$\sim Tr_3(33)$

$\sim Tr_4(33)$

$\vdots$

The first of our options here, the "true" option, licenses a list that contradicts that of (33) itself at an infinite number of points. In claiming both (33) and its truth, it appears, we would thus be committed to

$Tr_2(33)\ \&\ \sim Tr_2(33)$

$Tr_3(33)\ \&\ \sim Tr_3(33)$

$Tr_4(33)\ \&\ \sim Tr_4(33)$

$\vdots$

The option of claiming that (33) is false, on the other hand, seems to give us a subset of what (33) itself gives us. Not good. We would, moreover, be unable to maintain both the negation of (33) and the falsity of (33) without a similar infinite list of contradictions.[35]

Here let me also offer another form of the paradox, using the talk of schemata and their instances that Burge's account would seem to demand.

Consider the following:

Every instance of schema (35) is true.   (34)

$\sim Tr_i(34)$.   (35)

Now does the schema

$Tr_i(34)$

have a true instance or not? If it does have a true instance, (34) is false. If it has *no* true instance, on the other hand, it appears that (34) is simply true.[36]

So far I have concentrated on difficulties for Burge's approach to the Liar, but a similarly indexical-schematic approach can be imagined as a response to the Knower. Would this fare any better? Evidently not. In particular, if '$\triangle_i$' is to be iterable in the manner required for a genuinely global statement on the model of (32), we will continue to face a schematic form of the Knower.

Let us add '$\triangle_i$' to the language as a symbol required to express genuinely global claims regarding truth or knowledge in the manner that Burge outlines. Our system will now have the peculiarity that formulas containing '$\triangle_i$' will be read as schemata.

For some S, however, $S \equiv \triangle_i(\overline{\sim S})$ will be demonstrable in the system, as before. For '$\triangle_i$' as a representation of truth or knowledge, each of the schemata will once again seem inescapable:

$$\triangle_i(\overline{A}) \rightarrow A \tag{36}$$

$$\triangle_i((\overline{36})) \tag{37}$$

$$I(\overline{A}, \overline{B}) \rightarrow . \triangle_i(\overline{A}) \rightarrow \triangle_i(\overline{B}) \tag{38}$$

Here as before these will, of course, give us an explicit contradiction.

Burge's account, then, *were* it capable of schematically handling genuinely global claims regarding truth or knowledge, would fall victim to schematic forms of both the Liar and the Knower. Despite recourse to schemata, we are left with all the straightforward consequences of a simple hierarchy. Short of paradox, there will again be no level of statement or schemata on which one can genuinely speak of *all* truths. Short of paradox, a hierarchy for knowledge on the pattern Burge suggests would similarly leave no place for a true (39):

God knows all truths. (39)

Let me emphasize this last point. With a hierarchy of divine knowledge predicates $K_1, K_2, K_3, \ldots$, including perhaps a schematic $K_i, K_{i+1}, K_{i+2}, \ldots$, each claim C that God knows such and such will use a knowledge predicate of a certain level. But if any such claim is true, that C is *known* will be expressible only by means of a higher knowledge predicate. Given hierarchical restrictions crucial to avoid paradox, C cannot be claimed to be known within the scope of C itself. No such knowledge predicate, then, will be adequate to express omniscience.

With indices read as indicating times or persons, of course, this tells us that within a hierarchical account all truths cannot be said to be known at any time or by any person. Will it help for theological purposes to construe indices as "orders of knowledge" of some more occult sort? No order of God's knowledge exhausts omniscience, one might propose, but the *series* of his orders does.[37]

But even this won't do. For the proposal is in effect that we take 'is known within the series' as a new global knowledge predicate. Using 'K_Ω' to represent 'is known within the series', we get a form of the Liar with

$$\sim K_\Omega(40). \tag{40}$$

If (40) is known within the series, it is true, and thus it is not so known. But if it is not known within the series, it is true, and thus some truth is excluded from K_Ω. With 'K_Ω' as a global knowledge predicate we also get the Knower in full force.

Our choice once again, then, is between the contradictions of the paradoxes and abandonment of a genuinely global notion. In the case of knowledge that global notion is omniscience.

8 Conclusion

The paradox of the Knower poses a direct and formal challenge to the coherence of common notions of knowledge and truth. I have considered a number of ways one might try to met that challenge: propositional views of truth and knowledge, redundancy or operator views, and an appeal to hierarchy. Appeal to propositions or operators alone, however, seems insufficient against the Knower, at least if unsupplemented by an auxiliary recourse to hierarchy. But the cost of hierarchy, if adequate to handle paradox in other regards, appears to be abandonment of any notion of *all* truth or of total knowledge. What the contradictions of the Knower seem to demand, then, is at least an abandonment of these.

The ultimate lessons of the Knower, I think, are thus precisely those sketched in terms of the Liar in chapter one: that there can be no coherent notion of a set of all truths, of possible worlds construed in terms of maximal consistent sets of propositions, or of omniscience. Here as there, of course, one might continue to hope for a hidden way out—some new response or some new variation on an old one. But taken together, the Liar and the Knower do make a compelling case. As indicated in the next chapter, a similar case can also be made using relatives of Gödel's results.

3 Epistemic Incompleteness

In this chapter, as in its predecessors, what is ultimately at stake is a set of issues in epistemology and metaphysics, issues including the coherence of a notion of all truth, of certain conceptions of possible worlds, and of a notion of total knowledge. For purposes of exposition, however, I want to concentrate here on some questions regarding knowledge in particular.

Bodies of knowledge, or of what an individual knows, can, it seems, be conceived of on the model of something like formal systems. But if so, what do limitative results such as Gödel's incompleteness theorem have to tell us about the possibility of a *complete* body of knowledge? In terms evocative of the philosophy of religion, what do such results have to tell us about the possibility of omniscience?

In the first section that follows, I review the standard Gödel result with an eye to formal systems as models of ideal knowers or bodies of knowledge.[1] In section 2, I review some intriguing work on nonconstructive systems from a similar perspective. For the most part, however, these sections serve merely as a background review of relevant work. Though they do serve to illustrate the basic idea of systems as models of knowledge, it is perhaps a foregone conclusion that the inherent limitations of the systems considered in these sections will prohibit them from serving as anything like models of what a genuinely *omniscient* being would have to know.

In section 3, however, I attempt to broaden the notion of a system in a way that will free it from such limitations. Could any system in this *broader* sense model omniscience? A quite general Cantorian argument for what I term 'expressive incompleteness' seems to indicate that the answer even here is no.

In section 4, I sketch a more strictly Gödelian argument for a similar conclusion. Any system adequate as a model for omniscience would have to satisfy certain minimal requirements. But any system that satisfies those requirements—so the argument goes—will necessarily prove incomplete.

Variations on such incompleteness arguments, I suggest, offer an intriguing case against the coherence of any notion of total knowledge or of an omniscient mind. Here, as before, related conclusions would apply to a notion of a totality of truths and to any conception of possible worlds as maximal sets of propositions.

1 Some Ideal Knowers and the Standard Gödel Result

Many a body of knowledge, at least ideally, can be thought of on the model of an interpreted formal system. To the admissible formulas of the system, on such an analogy, will correspond all statements in the general domain of the body of knowledge, true or false, known or unknown. Formulas interpreted as basic truths or basic items of knowledge can be taken as axioms, and formulas interpreted as derivative truths, given appropriate transformation rules, will appear as theorems.[2] Here axiomatic geometries are, of course, prime examples. But given a liberal enough attitude toward sets of axioms, types of transformation rules, and the like, it appears that almost any familiar body of knowledge might be conceived of on the model of a formal system.[3]

If bodies of knowledge might be so conceived, might not *knowers*? Here we need not think that processes of knowledge acquisition or patterns of epistemic justification must somehow correspond to demonstrations within a formal system. Might not at least *what* a knower knows, the mere content of his knowledge, be conceived of on the model of a formal system?[4]

There *is* a major obstacle here, at least for familiar types of knowers and familiar types of systems. A formal system contains as a theorem every formula obtainable from its axioms by its specified transformation rules. If the transformation rules of such a system correspond to standard patterns of logical inference, then a corresponding knower would have to know, as derivative truths, every truth derivable from his basic items of knowledge. None of us is such a knower.[5]

This is precisely the difficulty noted in the previous chapter with regard to Hintikka's epistemic logic in *Knowledge and Belief* (1967). Within such a logic, given any $p \to q$ valid in ordinary propositional logic, we are committed to

$Kap \to Kaq,$

where 'Kap' is initially glossed as 'a knows that p'.[6] But this, of course, does not hold for ordinary knowers, who may well not know everything that follows from what they know.

As noted in chapter 2, Hintikka's original response to the problem was as follows: "Our results are not directly applicable to what is true or false in the actual world of ours. They tell us something definite about the truth and falsity of statements only in a world in which everybody follows the consequences of what he knows as far as they lead him" (Hintikka 1967, 36).[7]

On this approach, then, Hintikka's knowers are *ideal* knowers. The same might be said for the knowers envisaged above, those modelable by formal systems. Ideal knowers modelable by systems with transformation rules that correspond to standard patterns of logical inference in particular will know all logical consequences of what they know.[8] This limitation to ideal knowers is not the worrisome constraint for my purposes that it's commonly held to be for Hintikka's, however. For here *ideal* knowers, including omniscient knowers, are centrally at issue.

Let us start, then, by constructing in imagination an ideal knower whose knowledge can be conceived of on the model of a fairly standard formal system G. The transformation rules of G, let us suppose, do include on interpretation all standard rules of logical inference, and thus our ideal knower will know all that follows from what he knows. Let us also assume G to be standard in other regards: to contain a merely denumerable alphabet, for example, only finite formulas, and rules of inference restricted to finite sets of premises.

What of the basic knowledge of such a knower, corresponding to the axioms of G? Here we might insist that the axioms of G be finite. Instead, however, let us impose the weaker requirement that the axioms of G be recursively enumerable.

Were we to try to construct such a knower with as comprehensive a knowledge as possible, we would, of course, have to give him at least a working knowledge of number theory. Let us thus suppose all statements of number theory to be expressible in the language of system G and include within G axioms adequate for predicate calculus with identity and elementary arithmetic. With an eye to the latter, our axioms might, for example, include those for system Q of Robinson arithmetic, outlined in the preceding chapter. To give our ideal knower a fully comprehensive knowledge, of course, we'd also expect to build in much more: a million basic principles of physics, perhaps, a googolplex of basic principles of biochemistry, and an infinite (though still recursively enumerable) set of basic principles of psychology.

The lesson of Gödel's incompleteness theorem, however, is that no matter how much basic knowledge we imagine building into an ideal knower of this basic form—no matter what else is included among the recursively enumerable axioms of G—such a knower could never approach omniscience. If such a knower knows enough to handle basic number theory, in fact—no matter what *else* he knows—he already knows too *much* to know everything. At that point he already knows too much, in fact, to know the truth regarding all statements he can *express*—all statements in the language of *G* and thus, on our analogy, all statements in the general domain of his body of knowledge.

Somewhat more standardly expressed, the Gödel result is as follows. Any formal system with recursively recognizable formulas and axioms, with rules of inference from only finite sets of premises, and adequate at least for the general purposes of number theory, if consistent, will be incomplete.[9] Syntactically put, for some formula expressible in such a system, neither that formula nor its negation will appear as a theorem. Semantically put, any such system will fail to capture some truth of number theory as a theorem.

The Gödel result relies essentially just on the possibility of Gödel numbering for formulas of a system and the introduction of substitution and proof predicates. Gödel numbering for system *G* is assured simply by the fact that the alphabet of *G* is denumerable and the formulas of *G* are finite. Given Gödel numbering and axioms adequate for number theory, a substitution predicate can be introduced, and since the axioms of *G* are recursively enumerable and its rules of inference operate on only finite sets of premises, a proof predicate as well. These are in essence all we need to construct an undecidable sentence for *G*, a sentence that if *G* is consistent, demonstrably cannot appear as a theorem—and so cannot represent anything our ideal knower knows—and yet *does* represent a number-theoretical truth.[10] The knowledge of any ideal knower modelable by a system with the general configuration of *G*, no matter what we choose to include among the axioms of *G* in other regards, will then inevitably prove incomplete.

A similar incompleteness result will hold for any improved model of an ideal knower we attempt to construct, as long as the basic constraints on the general structure of *G* remain. In the attempt to envisage a more comprehensive knower, it is tempting, for example, to try to fill in system *G*'s "missing truth" by adding the undecidable sentence *S* as an axiom. But, of course, system *G* + *S* will prove incomplete as well. For *G* + *S*, we will be able to construct a new undecidable sentence *S'* in precisely the same way as before. For system *G* + *S* + *S'* there will in turn be an undecidable sentence *S''*, and so forth.[11] Here it might be tempting to try to add as axioms an infinite series of missing truths, or an infinite series of infinite series. As long as what we add remains recursively enumerable, however, the basic mechanisms of the Gödel result will still be in play, and any improved system we build will still be provably incomplete. The strategy of adding infinite series of infinite series of previously "missing" truths in fact ultimately leads one to a progression that corresponds to that of the constructive ordinals. At that point we've reached the outside limit of systems with the basic structure specified for G: by a result due to Church and Kleene, there is no recursively related notation scheme adequate even for *naming* each of the constructive ordinals.[12]

If we take the basic restrictions on G as defining standard systems, all standard systems are essentially incomplete.[13] The knowers to which they correspond, however ideal in other regards, will be essentially nonomniscient.

2 Beyond Standard Systems

The ideal knowers we've envisaged so far correspond to standard formal systems adequate for number theory—systems standard in the sense of having a denumerable alphabet, formulas of only finite length, recursively enumerable axioms, and rules of inference from only finitely many premises.

On the grounds of Gödel's standard incompleteness theorem, no such ideal knower can be omniscient. But, of course, God *is* standardly conceived of as omniscient. So God, if there be such a being, must not be an ideal knower of this kind.

Should this be considered a negative theological conclusion? Not necessarily. The work of the preceding section might instead be considered a positive theological contribution in the spirit of the *via negativa*, an approach to God by way of an understanding of what he is not. God's knowledge is quite standardly said, for example, to be infinite. But this would clearly be inadequate as a characterization of omniscience, since the knowledge of many an ideal knower of merely the lowly sort considered in the preceding section will be literally infinite. *God's* knowledge would have to be much *more* than merely infinite; it would have to be a knowledge essentially incapable of being captured at all within the systematic confines outlined above. Some have argued in effect that these confines are our confines as well, that the limits of standard formal systems are also the limits of the human mind.[14] If so, the conclusions above might properly be welcomed in theological circles as a particularly precise vindication of the doctrine that a divine mind would have to be essentially different in kind from our own.

But what lies beyond such standard systems? What happens, for instance, if we weaken one or more of the constraints imposed on systems and on corresponding knowers? That is a question for which no general and exhaustive answer can be said to exist. The systematic constraints of section 1 are in essence the limitations of constructive methods themselves, and to violate those constraints is thus to leave constructive methods behind. Beyond such constraints formal systems cease to be genuinely formal at all, and conceptions of proof and demonstration must change at the border. Beyond lies not logic in the familiar sense but what Geoffrey Hellman has appropriately termed 'theologic' (1981).

Important attempts to go beyond standard systems have been made, however. Here I want to offer a brief survey of some important contributions, though it will perhaps come as no surprise that inherent limitations of even such nonconstructive systems render them ultimately unsuitable as models for any genuinely comprehensive knowledge or any genuinely omniscient being.[15]

Carnap appears to have been the first to propose relaxing that condition that limits rules of inference to finite premises, introducing instead a nonconstructive rule of inference from $f(0)$, $f(1)$, $f(2)$, ... to $\forall x(f(x))$. Barkley Rosser considered systems allowing up to ω^2 uses of such a rule. Within that limitation, however, systems still prove incomplete in the standard ways: each system still contains an undecidable sentence and a consistency formula unprovable in the system (Rosser 1937).

Such an approach is taken further in a system S_∞ developed in various forms by G. Gentzen, W. Ackerman, P. Lorenzen, K. Schütte, and I. Hlodovskii. 'Proof' within S_∞ is redefined in terms of proof trees. To each formula of a proof tree an ordinal is assigned so that the result of applying a weak rule of the system is given the same ordinal as its premise and the result of applying a strong rule or cut is given an ordinal greater than that of its premises.[16] Restriction on the ordinals assignable to the formulas of proof trees restricts the notion of proof accordingly. But if *no* restriction is placed on the class of ordinals that can be attached to proofs, we get a system that, though highly nonconstructive, is consistent, ω-consistent, and complete (Mendelson 1964, 270).

This might make it appear as if some genuinely comprehensive system, modeling a genuinely comprehensive knower, could escape the curse of Gödel on the wings of transfinite induction. But here some important limitations of S_∞ should be noted. First of all, the proof of consistency for S_∞ is not internally formalizable. As Gentzen himself showed, transfinite induction up to ε_0 cannot itself be formalized within S_∞.[17] A second difficulty is perhaps even more telling for our purposes. S_∞, obtained from a more standard number theory S by the addition of a rule permitting transfinite induction, is still capable of dealing only with finite sets. For systems dealing with infinite sets as well—a clear prerequisite for any system taken to model a genuinely comprehensive knowledge—even transfinite induction will not be enough. Such systems will still prove incomplete.[18]

A different nonconstructive approach, closely related to Turing's 1938 "ordinal logics," appears in Solomon Feferman's work on transfinite sequences of recursively enumerable axiom systems.[19]

Starting with an initial axiom system A_0, we envisage a progression of systems in terms of the ordinals. At each successor ordinal we apply a succession principle such as (1).

$$A_{k+1} = A_k \cup \{\mathrm{Con}_{A_k}\}, \tag{1}$$

where Con_{A_k} is a formula expressing the consistency of A_k. At each limit ordinal A_k, we take the union $\bigcup_{i<k} A_k$.

Consider, then, the theorems of an entire progression of axiom systems of this sort. Might not these offer a promise of completeness?

So it might seem. Feferman notes that a general incompleteness result for such progressions, regardless of the successor principle chosen, would have been dramatic proof of the far-reaching extent of incompleteness phenomena. "However, the situation has not turned out this way" (Feferman 1962, 261). For progressions based on a particular principle of succession, all true statements of number theory *are* provable in the progression. It is possible, moreover, to choose a path through the constructive ordinals along which all theorems of the progression are provable.[20]

Once again, however, it would be rash to think that crucial limitations have been overcome. Most important for my purposes is perhaps the simple fact that the attractive completeness of Feferman's progressions is lost for progressions based on higher than first-order calculi. Here Feferman does in fact demonstrate a quite general incompleteness result:

for any consistent progression based on at least the second-order calculus, there is either a true Π_1^1 or a true Σ_1^1 sentence that is not provable from $\bigcup_{d \in O} A_d$ (Feferman 1962, 314).

Here let me finally mention R. G. Jeroslow's "experimental logics" (Jeroslow 1975; see also Hajek 1977). These transcend the limits of standard systems in being interpretable in effect as dynamic rather than static, as progressively building over time. As such a logic develops, axioms and even rules of inference can be withdrawn or supplemented. Thus, in a sense, experimental logics offer models not merely of ideal knowers but also of ideal learners.[21]

Such logics don't seem to offer any bright hope for modeling a developmental march toward a genuinely comprehensive knowledge, however. Jeroslow terms an experimental logic *convergent* if its recurring formulas do not vacillate indefinitely, if eventually "the conceptual superstructure settles down" (Jeroslow 1975, 256). To model an (eventually) omniscient being, then, we would need a logic that converged on all truths, on at least, say, all truths of the form $\forall x(R(x))$ for R recursive. But this does not appear to be possible. For logics at issue, Jeroslow has shown that the joint requirements of consistency, convergence, and closure under reasoning are in fact inconsistent with the goal of obtaining all truths $\forall x(R(x))$ (Jeroslow 1975, 257, 264–265).

Each of the approaches above does take us beyond the constructive limitations of standard systems in some intriguing way. Nonetheless, each still carries internal limitations bound to make it unsuitable as a model for a comprehensive knowledge or a comprehensive knower.

Is that enough, together with the results of section 1, to show that *no* system could serve as such a model? That would clearly be too strong. The standard Gödel result stops at the limit of standard systems, and what I have offered here is merely a sample of some important nonconstructive attempts.

In the next section I want to consider an argument that does appear to offer a more general negative result: that *no* system, in a very free sense of that term, can serve as a model for total knowledge or for omniscience.

3 Expressive Incompleteness

The knowledge of an omniscient being can correspond to no system yet considered. But we have not yet shown that it can correspond to no system at all.

A quite simple but powerful Cantorian argument seems to show just that. For at least a particular type of incompleteness—what I will term 'expressive incompleteness'—*any* system meeting certain minimal conditions will prove incomplete. Those minimal conditions would seem clearly necessary in any system intended to model omniscience. But no system that meets those conditions can be complete, and no *in*complete system can model omniscience. To the knowledge of an omniscient being, it appears, can correspond no system at all.

It should perhaps be emphasized that what follows is not a form of Gödel's argument and that expressive incompleteness is not incompleteness in the standard sense. A Cantorian generalization of a related but more strictly Gödelian incompleteness result is offered in section 4.

It should also perhaps be noted that the general argument for expressive incompleteness is in a sense philosophical rather than formal. The core of the result is a very general characteristic of systems in a very general sense, and that generality can all too easily be obscured by an unduly limited or conventional specification of the systems at issue.[22]

To introduce some basic ideas, it's helpful to begin with an example in mind. Let us start, therefore, with a proof of expressive incompleteness for a familiar type of system.

Consider again standard formal systems of number theory. Basic strings of symbols within such systems correspond on interpretation to the natural numbers, and it is these that such systems are taken to be *about*. Fairly intuitively, then, the natural numbers are what I will term the *objects* of such systems. Within such systems also appear formulas of one variable, which in accordance with common parlance I will call *predicates*.[23]

Now suppose such a system with the following characteristics:

1. It can in some way take each predicate expressible in the language of the system as an object. A system with this capacity I will term *self-reflective*, for fairly obvious reasons. Standard systems of number theory are, of course, self-reflective by virtue of Gödel numbering: each predicate can be encoded as an object of the system.[24]

2. The system is designed to be capable of at least expressing all properties of its objects—for systems immediately at issue, all properties of the natural numbers.[25]

The essential difficulty is this: conditions (1) and (2) cannot both be satisfied. For consider the following questions: How many objects would be at issue for such a system? How many properties of individual objects? How many expressible predicates?[26]

There must first of all be at least as many objects of such a system as there are predicates within it, since each predicate can be taken as an object. The device of Gödel numbering, for example, assigns a distinct number to each open formula of one variable, and thus there must be at least as many numbers, the objects of such a system, as there are predicates within it.

But there must also be more *properties* of individual objects of the system than there are individual objects. Consider the set of objects of the system—numbers, in this case—which we might envisage as the set O:

$$O = \{o_1, o_2, o_3, \ldots\}$$

For the moment let us treat properties purely extensionally, so that possession of distinct properties will amount merely to membership in distinct sets. Extensionally construed, then, properties of objects of the system at issue will correspond to subsets of the set of objects, to elements of the power set $\mathscr{P}O$. We might envisage a listing of such properties as follows:[27]

P^1, corresponding to $\varnothing$

P^2, corresponding to $\{o_1\}$

P^3, corresponding to $\{o_2\}$

P^4, corresponding to $\{o_3\}$

$$\vdots$$

P'^1, corresponding to $\{o_1, o_2\}$

P'^2, corresponding to $\{o_1, o_3\}$

$$\vdots$$

P''^1, corresponding to $\{o_1, o_2, o_3\}$

$$\vdots$$

A purely extensional treatment of properties of this sort is, of course, extremely artificial. Properties are more properly thought of intensionally, and so conceived, any number of coextensive properties might correspond to each of the sets above. This richer set of properties intensionally construed, however, is not in fact required for the argument at hand. For the moment we can simply note that for properties intensionally construed a list like that above would be merely partial.

Even if construed purely extensionally, then, there will be as many properties applicable to individual objects of any system at issue as there are elements in the power set of objects of that system. But by Cantor's power set theorem, we know that the power set of any set is larger than the set itself.[28] There must therefore be more properties applicable to individual objects of such a system than there are objects themselves.

By the first part of the argument, then, for any system of the sort specified, there will be as many objects of the system—numbers, in this case—as expressible predicates. But by the second part of the argument, there must be more properties of individual objects than objects themselves.

For any such system, therefore, there will be more properties of individual objects of the system than there will be appropriate predicates with which to express them. Properties will outnumber corresponding predicates. Some genuine property of the objects of any self-reflective system must therefore go unexpressed, and thus condition (2), that each property of its objects be at least expressible in the system, cannot be satisfied. It follows that some *truth* regarding an object of the system, that it does (or does not) have a particular property, will be incapable even of *expression* in the system. All such systems will be expressively incomplete.[29]

As just presented, of course, the argument for expressive incompleteness is still tied to particular features of familiar formal systems. Here I have taken numbers as the objects of systems at issue and open formulas of one variable as predicates, and I have appealed to the device of Gödel numbering in thinking of such systems as taking their own predicates as objects.

The general argument will hold, however, for any system interpreted as applying to a domain of objects—those things the system is taken to be about—and including a range of predicates applicable in the system. If any such system is self-reflective—if each of its predicates can in some sense be taken as an object to which the system applies—it will have at least as many objects as predicates. But even if we take properties purely extensionally, by Cantor's power set theorem there will be more properties of individual objects of the system than corresponding predicates with which to express them. Some genuine property of objects of the system, and thus some truth, will be inexpressible; any such system will prove expressively incomplete. Expressive incompleteness, then, is by no means limited to standard formal systems; it will apply to any system that meets the basic condition of self-reflection.

No system, it appears, can model omniscience. For any system intended as such a model would surely have to include its own predicates among the objects it is interpreted as being about; any such system would have to be self-reflective. But any self-reflective system, we've seen, will be expressively incomplete: some property of its objects, and thus some truth, will be incapable even of expression within the system.

Note also how very thin a notion of system is in fact required here. Nothing in the basic argument requires that any system at issue be formal or constructive in any way. Nothing in the basic argument requires, for that matter, that any system at issue be axiomatic in form or even that it be construed as offering a set of theorems.

All the argument requires, in fact, is a system of expression—in a word, a language. The basic result here might then be put as follows. Given even minimal requirements of expressive self-reflection, any system of *expression* must prove expressively incomplete. In that sense, there could not even be a *language* adequate for the expression of all truths.

One clear application of such an argument will be against any notion of a divine language. In a different context, for example, Michael Loux notes that a basic obstacle for any Aristotelian attempt to treat such abstract objects as propositions and properties in terms of sentences, utterances, or predicates is the fact that "our language has limitations of an obvious and familiar sort. As the Platonist wants to put it, there are more propositions than declarative sentences and more attributes than predicates for characterizing, classifying and relating objects" (Loux 1986, 508). Loux's solution is to propose that such an Aristotelian reduction *would* hold for God's language. "Suppose, however, that God were to use a language. Call it Godspeak." Since Godspeak "would have sufficient descriptive resources to permit an exhaustive characterization of the divine mental life," Loux proposes, propositions and properties *could* essentially be reduced to sentences and propositions of *that* language.

As an Aristotelian, I would make the point by saying that our predicate-resources for characterizing God's mental life are outstripped by that mental life, and it is precisely this fact, I want to claim, that makes it necessary for us to speak of propositions, properties, and the like. Were we to have at our disposal the descriptive resources sufficient to express all the ways God is in God's conceiving, entertaining, and believing, talk of the various abstract entities would be dispensable.

On the basis of the Cantorian argument above, however, it appears that any divine language of the sort Loux envisages must itself be impossible. The important point is that it is not merely familiar human languages that will fail to capture all properties as predicates or all propositions as sentences. Given any self-reflective language capable of taking each of its predicates as objects—a clear requisite for Godspeak, for example, which is envisaged as having "sufficient descriptive resources to permit an exhaustive characterization of the divine mental life"—there will be some property not captured as a predicate and some proposition not captured as a sentence. An Aristotelian linguistic reduction is clearly not to be salvaged by appeal to a provably impossible language.

In the end, however, the work above can also be construed as more than just an argument that there can be no system and no language adequate for omniscience. It can be construed as an argument that the notion of an omniscient mind must itself be incoherent.

The most direct way to make such an argument is to rephrase the Cantorian argument above in terms of features that would be required of an omniscient mind. In place of predicates, for example, let us speak of conceptions of properties. For the moment I will use 'objects of knowledge' to indicate those things that a knower knows something about.

Any omniscient mind would surely be self-reflective in at least the following sense: among its objects of knowledge, among those things it knows something about, would be its own conceptions of properties. But here we can simply rephrase the argument above to show that the knowledge of no such mind could be complete. Any such mind will have at least as many objects of knowledge as conceptions of properties, since each of the latter will also be an object of knowledge. But by Cantor's power set theorem, there will be more actual properties of its objects of knowledge than objects themselves. Actual properties will outnumber its conceptions of properties. Thus some genuine property of its objects of knowledge, and therefore some truth, will fall outside even its range of *conception*.

An omniscient mind, so the argument goes, would have to be self-reflective in the sense specified. But no self-reflective mind can be omniscient. There can then be no omniscient mind.

4 A Cantorian Generalization of Gödel's Incompleteness Theorem

The argument above is not Gödel's argument, I noted, and expressive incompleteness is not the form that incompleteness takes in his work.

Expressive incompleteness is a pervasive limitation on what can even be expressed within a system. What Gödel showed, phrased in semantic form, is rather that for a wide range of systems, on the assumption of consistency, some formula that *is* expressible in the system and represents a truth on interpretation nonetheless cannot be captured as a theorem. This more familiar form we might term *internal* incompleteness.

These two forms of incompleteness are not coextensive; internal incompleteness holds for only a somewhat more restricted class of systems than does expressive incompleteness. In the spirit of the preceding section, however, a quite general Cantorian argument for internal incompleteness can also be constructed, an argument that offers some philosophical indication of how far beyond the restrictions of standard formal systems even Gödelian incompleteness will apply.[30]

Here let us start, as before, with a self-reflective system, one capable of taking each of its expressible predicates as an object. For any such system, consider the set P of expressible predicates,

$$P = \{P^1, P^2, P^3, \ldots\},$$

and the corresponding set O_P of *predicate objects*, those objects of the system that are its expressible predicates taken as objects:

$$O_P = \{o_{P^1}, o_{P^2}, o_{P^3}, \ldots\}.$$

Clearly these two sets will be the same size: there will be a one-to-one function f that maps each predicate object o_P onto some expressible predicate $f(o_P)$ and such that some predicate object is mapped onto each expressible predicate. An obvious candidate for such a function, of course, would be one that maps each predicate object onto the predicate of which it *is* the corresponding object. Many other functions would satisfy the conditions on f as well, however.[31]

For any such function f, consider any individual predicate object o_P and its associated predicate $f(o_P)$. That predicate may or may not in fact apply to the object at issue; a formula we might think of as $f(o_P)o_P$, in other words, may or may not represent a *truth* on the intended interpretation. Also, $f(o_P)o_P$ may or may not appear as a *theorem* within the system.[32]

For any choice of f, then, consider the following set:

$$O'_P = \{o_P \mid f(o_P)o_P \text{ is not a theorem}\}$$

O'_p is, of course, explicitly just a set of objects of the system, and in that regard it might seem a plausible candidate for the extension of a predicate. Such a predicate would apply to precisely those objects that are members of O'_p: to all and only predicate objects o_p for which $f(o_p)o_p$ does not appear as a theorem.

The crucial question here is this: is such a predicate expressible in the system, or not? If not, of course, the system will be expressively impoverished in certain respects. But if such a predicate *is* expressible for any f of the sort indicated, then if the system at issue is also consistent, it must prove internally incomplete. Some truth expressible in the system will not be captured as a theorem.

Suppose that for some f such a predicate *is* expressible in the system. Since f is taken as mapping a predicate object o_p onto each predicate expressible in the system, f must then map some o_p onto *this* predicate.

But consider any object o_p^* taken as filling such a role: any object o_p^* such that $f(o_p^*)$ has extension O'_p. Will $f(o_p^*)$ in fact apply to o_p^* or not? We have two options:

Suppose first that the predicate at issue will *not* apply to its associated object. Here I bring in the final assumption, that of consistency, in the following form: that only truths on the intended interpretation will appear as theorems within the system.[33] On the supposition that the predicate at issue will not apply to its associated object, then, the formula $f(o_p^*)o_p^*$ will not be a theorem. The predicate at issue, however, is specified as having O'_p as its extension and thus as applying to every predicate object o_p for which $f(o_p)o_p$ is not a theorem. Contrary to our initial negative assumption, then, we are forced to conclude that the predicate at issue *will* apply to its associated object.

Suppose, then, that the predicate at issue *does* apply to its associated object o_p^*. In that case $f(o_p^*)o_p^*$ will represent a truth. The predicate at issue, however, has been specified as applying only to those objects o_p for which $f(o_p)o_p$ is not a theorem. Since the predicate at issue does apply to its corresponding o_p^* in this case, that is, since $f(o_p^*)o_p^*$ is true, it is also the case that $f(o_p^*)o_p^*$ is not a theorem.

At least one truth expressible in any such system, then, will not be captured as a theorem. Any such system must be internally incomplete.

The argument can be repeated for any choice of a one-to-one function f that assigns to each expressible predicate a corresponding object; for any such f there will be a predicate that, if expressible in the system, will give us the same result. Despite the surface complexities of the argument, then, the assumptions required are genuinely minimal: the system at issue must be self-reflective, consistent, and capable of expressing at least one of a range of predicates specified in terms of their extensions.

Note also that although the argument concerns systems conceived of as having objects of some sort, expressible predicates, and theorems, little else has been said to restrict that class of systems to which it will apply. In particular, nothing has been said to limit relevant systems to anything like those meeting standard formal constraints.[34]

How general, then, is the phenomenon of incompleteness? Expressive incompleteness, we've seen, will hold for any self-reflective system. Internal incompleteness can be said to hold for any self-reflective and consistent system capable of expressing any of a range of particular predicates.

Here a bit more should perhaps be said, at least informally, about how little expressive capacity is actually required in the latter regard. Just two conditions will basically suffice:

• The system is interpretable as expressing the notion that a formula is or is not a theorem.

• At least one function f is expressible that maps an object o_p onto each expressible predicate $f(o_p)$.

Given essentially these two conditions, a predicate can be constructed with extension O'_p, and given such a predicate, any self-reflective and consistent system will also prove internally incomplete.

Let us return at this point to the analogy between systems and knowers, and in particular to the analogy between systems and the notion of an omniscient knower. In the preceding section I outlined an argument against the possibility of an omniscient mind based on the phenomenon of expressive incompleteness. Internal incompleteness, I noted, applies to a somewhat more restricted class of systems. But is there also a more strictly Gödelian argument against the possibility of omniscience lurking in the phenomenon of internal incompleteness? Yes.

An omniscient mind must be self-reflective in at least the sense of being able to take its conceptions of properties as themselves objects of knowledge. But one might also argue that any genuinely omniscient mind will have to be self-aware in deeper senses as well. Among the things that an omniscient mind will know, of course, is that it knows certain things, and thus in general it will be able to conceive of its knowing something or not. Such a mind, one might insist, will surely also be cognizant of obvious aspects of its own conceptual structure. It will, for example, be aware of one-to-one mappings between its conceptions of properties and these conceptions taken self-reflectively as objects of knowledge.

Omniscience, then—so the argument goes—would have formal features analogous to those outlined for systems above: self-reflectivity and expressibility of both theoremhood and some one-to-one function f between predicates and predicate objects within the system. The knowledge of any omniscient mind would, of course, also be consistent. But any *system* with these formal features will prove internally incomplete: some truth expressible in the system will not be captured as a theorem. For essentially the same reasons, it appears, the knowledge of any being proposed as omniscient must be correspondingly incomplete: there will be some truth that *is* within the range of its conception and yet will *not* appear among the things it knows.

This more Gödelian argument, it must be admitted, does demand more points of comparison between systems and knowers. Since internal incompleteness applies for a more restricted class of systems than does expressive incompleteness, moreover, it will apply to a smaller class of ideal knowers. What the argument suggests, however, is that any mind satisfying even minimal conditions necessary for omniscience would fall victim to two quite different forms of incompleteness. Given any self-reflective mind, some truth will lie beyond its range of conception—such is the lesson of expressive incompleteness. Given any mind self-aware in somewhat deeper regards, there will, moreover, be a truth within its range of conception that nonetheless does not appear among the things it knows.

5 Conclusion

Here I have tried to track the analogy between formal systems and ideal knowers or bodies of knowledge through a series of limiting results. That no standard formal system could model a genuinely comprehensive knowledge or a genuinely omniscient mind is perhaps not too surprising, and the fact that a range of attempts at nonconstructive systems face similar obstacles may be little more so. The phenomenon of expressive incompleteness, however, will extend to *any* self-reflective system in a very free sense of 'system'. And a more Gödelian internal incompleteness requires little more.

Both results seem to suggest quite fatal difficulties for the coherence of omniscience.

Here an objector might be expected to emphasize that all of this is built on the notion that ideal minds *are* in some sense analogous to formal systems or formal languages. Can we escape the force of arguments against omniscience above simply by renouncing that assumption?

I think not, for the simple reason that the notion of system at issue is ultimately so very thin and thus the analogy required is ultimately so trivial. The argument against omniscience from expressive incompleteness in particular can be phrased without reference to systems or languages at all. In the end, all that is required is that an omniscient being be assumed to know something about each of its conceptions of properties. Without that assumption it's far from clear that an omniscient *mind* can be at issue at all. We might also avoid the term 'conceptions' if we wish: a slight variation of the Cantorian argument requires only that an omniscient being know something about each of the properties it knows to be instantiated.[35] To abandon that assumption, it seems, would simply be to abandon the notion of an omniscient *knower* altogether.

In this chapter I have concentrated on issues phrased in terms of omniscience in particular. Just beneath the surface, however, lies the entire set of issues, metaphysical and epistemological, that has guided us throughout. A form of the arguments above will also hold, for example, against any notion of a totality of truths or any approach to possible worlds in terms of maximal sets of propositions.

If we envisage bodies of truths as systems broadly construed, any genuinely comprehensive body of truths would have to be self-reflective in roughly the following sense: any system at issue would have to include some truth regarding each property applied within the system, each property P for which there is a truth within the system to the effect that something is P. But for much the same reasons as before, any self-reflective body of truths will prove expressively incomplete: there will be some truth it does *not* include. If we envisage sets of propositions as systems, self-reflectiveness would similarly seem to prohibit any *maximal* consistent set. Though somewhat more complicated, arguments for internal incompleteness parallel to those offered above can be constructed in these cases as well. Despite my concentration here on the notion of omniscience, then, there will be arguments of essentially the same structure against any totality of truth and against any notion of possible worlds as maximal consistent sets of propositions.

In chapter four I want to consider a range of related arguments that avoid some of the complications courted here: a series of quite general Cantorian arguments that cut neatly through systems to sets.

4 Classes and Quantification: The Cantorian Argument

In chapters one through three I considered major difficulties posed by forms of the Liar, the Knower, and relatives of Gödel's result for a notion of universal knowledge or of a totality of truths. There is much to be said, I think, for the suspicion that what is at stake in all of these cases is in fact the *same* difficulty, though appearing in slightly different guises—the suspicion that there is a single deep problem regarding truth, knowledge, and totality that is simply visible in different forms in the Liar, the Knower, and Gödelian results.

If it is indeed the *same* problem that is at issue, what follows may be the cleanest and most concise form in which we have yet seen it. By a simple Cantorian argument, it appears, there can be no set of all truths.[1]

In what follows, I want to outline the essential argument against a set of all truths and then sketch some important extensions and applications. As in previous chapters, however, I also want to go on to consider possible replies. Here these include appeals to alternative set theories, requiring an extended excursion into a variety of treatments of classes. They also include an intriguing invocation of ZF − power—Zermelo-Fraenkel set theory without a power set axiom—proposed by Christopher Menzel. In each of these cases the basic Cantorian argument seems to emerge victorious: with or without the power set axiom, it appears, there can be neither a set, a class, nor a totality of all truths.

The strongest reply may be one that grants the central thesis of the chapter—that there can be no set or other collection of all truths or all propositions—but that insists nonetheless that we can unproblematically *quantify* over them all. Though there may be no single totality of truths or propositions, can't we nonetheless speak *quantificationally* of all truths or all propositions? In section 5, I introduce a series of Cantorian arguments that suggest that even here the answer may be no, that in the end even the notion of universal propositional quantification itself may fall victim to the type of argument we've tracked throughout. In section 6, I consider the implications of such an argument for our understanding even of the central conclusion that there can be no set of all truths.

1 There Is No Set of All Truths

The proof that there can be no set of all truths is as follows. Suppose there *is* a set of all truths T:

$$T = \{t_1, t_2, t_3, \ldots\}$$

And consider further all subsets of T, elements of the power set $\mathscr{P}T$:

$\varnothing$

$\{t_1\}$

$\{t_2\}$

$\{t_3\}$

$\vdots$

$\{t_1, t_2\}$

$\{t_1, t_3\}$

$\vdots$

$\{t_1, t_2, t_3\}$

$\vdots$

To each element of this power set there will correspond a truth. To each set of the power set, for example, t_1 either will or will not belong as a member. In either case we will have a truth:[2]

$t_1 \notin \varnothing$

$t_1 \in \{t_1\}$

$t_1 \notin \{t_2\}$

$t_1 \notin \{t_3\}$

$\vdots$

$t_1 \in \{t_1, t_2\}$

$t_1 \in \{t_1, t_3\}$

$\vdots$

$t_1 \in \{t_1, t_2, t_3\}$

$\vdots$

There will then be at least as many truths as there are elements of the power set $\mathscr{P}T$. But by Cantor's power set theorem the power set of any set will be *larger* than the original. There will then be *more* truths than there are members of T; some truths will be left out.

Though I have appealed to the power set theorem before, it is perhaps worth a moment to exhibit the full Cantorian argument phrased specifically in terms of sets and truths.[3]

Were there only as many elements of the power set $\mathscr{P}T$ as members of T itself, there would be some one-to-one function f that assigned each member t of T to some set $f(t)$ of $\mathscr{P}T$ and such that to each element of $\mathscr{P}T$ some member of T was assigned. Suppose, then, any one-to-one function f from T to $\mathscr{P}T$, and consider the following subset of T:

$$T' = \{t: t \notin f(t)\},$$

the set of just those members t of T that are not members of the set in $\mathscr{P}T$ assigned them by the chosen function f.

T' is itself quite clearly an element of $\mathscr{P}T$. But what element t of T can the function f assign to it? Consider any t in T.

If that t is a member of T', it is *not* a member of its associated $f(t)$: T' contains as members only those t that are not members of their associated set $f(t)$. If t is a member of T', it is not a member of its $f(t)$, and so T' cannot be that set assigned to it as its $f(t)$.

If our chosen t is *not* a member of T', on the other hand, it *will* be a member of its associated $f(t)$: T' excludes only those t that *are* members of their associated sets. If t is not a member of T', it is a member of its associated $f(t)$, and so again T' cannot be the set assigned to it as its $f(t)$.

In either case, then, t cannot be that element of T to which the set T' of $\mathscr{P}T$ corresponds as $f(t)$. But t was taken above as *any* member of T, and thus *no* member of T will be mapped onto T' by the chosen function. T' will simply be left out of the mapping f. The function f, however, was taken as any one-to-one function from T to $\mathscr{P}T$. Any such function will therefore leave out some element of $\mathscr{P}T$, that is, $\mathscr{P}T$ must be larger than T.

To each element of $\mathscr{P}T$, we've noted, there will correspond a truth. There will then be more truths than members of T, and for any set of truths T, there will be some truth left out. There can then be no set of *all* truths.

Here there need be no suggestion, by the way, that truths be thought of as *linguistic* entities in even the most attenuated or metaphorical sense. Nothing in the argument demands, for example, that the truths at issue be in any way linguistically expressible.[4] The result would thus be the same for 'true propositions', for 'actual states of affairs', or for 'facts' in place of 'truths': there can be no set of all true propositions, no set of all facts, and no set of all actual states of affairs.[5]

2 Extensions and Applications

Essentially the same Cantorian argument can be used to show that there can be no set of all falsehoods and that there can be no set of all propositions.

The argument can also be applied against the existence of "smaller" sets. Consider, for example, the set not of all truths but merely of all metamathematical truths. Is there such a set? Here we first have to answer a clarificatory question. Does each truth regarding the membership of a set of metamathematical truths itself qualify as a metamathematical truth? If so, we can construct a Cantorian argument to show that there can be no set of all metamathematical truths; each set of metamathematical truths will leave out some metamathematical truth.[6]

The same will hold for any set of truths of type Θ, where truths regarding membership in sets of truths of type Θ themselves qualify as truths of that type. For no such type of truths will there be a set of *all* truths of that type.[7]

In each form of the Cantorian argument appealed to so far, however, what we are asked to envisage is a *necessary* truth corresponding to each element of the power set at issue. For each element s of the power set T in the argument against a set of all truths, for example, we are asked to envisage a truth of the form $t_1 \in s$ or of the form $t_1 \notin s$—in either case a truth of set membership and so presumably a necessary truth. What this might suggest is that although there can be no set of all *necessary* truths, and for that reason there can be no set of *all* truths, there *could* nonetheless be a set of all *contingent* truths.[8]

Just as there can be no set of all truths, all falsehoods, or all propositions, however, there can be no set of all contingent truths, all contingent falsehoods, or all contingent propositions.

Suppose, for example, that there *were* a set T^c of all contingent truths, and consider its power set $\mathscr{P}T^c$, composed of sets s of contingent truths. Consider also any chosen contingent truth c. To each set s of the power set there will correspond a truth of one of the following forms, depending on whether c is or is not a member of s:

$c \ \& \ (c \in s)$,

$c \ \& \ (c \notin s)$.

If c is a member of s, since c is also a truth, the first of these will give us a truth. If c is not a member of s, on the other hand, the second of these will give us a truth. Thus in either case we will have a truth. In either case, moreover, we will have a *contingent* truth, since the conjunction of a contingent and a necessary proposition is itself contingent. There will then be more contingent truths than members of T^c, and thus T^c cannot be a set of all contingent truths. For essentially the same reasons, there will be no set of all contingent falsehoods or of all contingent propositions. If extensions are construed standardly in terms of sets, 'true', 'false', 'necessary', 'contingent', and 'is a proposition' simply have no extensions.

Can we at least hope for a set of all *atomic* contingent propositions? Even a set of atomic propositions, at least in any classical sense of atomism, seem to fall victim to Cantorian argument. Suppose a set A of all atomic propositions and a set c^* of all connectives. Within classical atomism compounds of these will give us all propositions. If A and c^* are sets, however, by standard set-theoretical principles, all compounds composed of elements of A and c^* will also form a set. We know independently that there can be no set of all propositions, and thus by *modus tollens* there can be no set of all classical atomic propositions.

Let us turn from extensions of the basic Cantorian result to philosophical applications. One thing the work above gives us is a shorter and simpler argument regarding omniscience—though at least initially a more conditional one—than those sketched in the preceding chapter. By definition, an omniscient being would have to know all truths. But there can be no set of all truths. Thus at the very least there can be no set of all that an omniscient being would have to know. *If* for any being there is a corresponding set of things it knows, there can be no omniscient being.

As J. H. Sobel has pointed out, such an argument can be constructed regarding even a *non*omniscient being of a certain sort.[9] For consider a being that, although perhaps not omniscient, does know *itself* very well: it knows (*de re*, let us say), for each set that contains only propositions that it knows, *that* the set contains only propositions that it knows. Consider now a set of all that such a being knows and the power set of that set. To each set of the power set there will correspond a proposition that this being, as specified, knows, namely, that the set consists only of propositions that it knows. But then, of course, there will be more propositions that such a being knows than are contained in the set of *all* that the being knows. On the assumption that what such a being knows would form a set, then, there could be no such being.

In both cases here the argument is phrased in terms of sets, and I have accordingly expressed conclusions conditionally: *if* what an omniscient being knows would form a set, there can be no omniscient being. The work of later sections indicates that the central difficulties at issue go well beyond sets, however. For present purposes, it is perhaps sufficient to note a form of the argument that avoids explicit mention of sets. Here I am indebted to David L. Boyer.

Assume that there is an omniscient God. Consider all that such a being would know, and consider further what would be known by each of a complete and maximal chorus of archangels, perhaps fictional, that would satisfy the following condition: each archangel knows something, no two archangels know precisely the same things, and for each archangel there is something that God knows and it does not. Let us also add two more "archangels," in a somewhat extended sense: an archangel who knows absolutely nothing, and God himself.[10]

Now for each of the archangels envisaged, there would be something that an omniscient being would know: that it is possible that such a being exists, perhaps, or that it is not possible; that the knowledge of that archangel would include the fact that seven is prime, perhaps, or that it would not. There will be, then, at least as many things God knows as there are envisaged archangels.

By the basic mechanism of the initial argument above, however, there will then be *more* archangels than things God knows. The initial assumption leads to contradiction and so must be abandoned: there can be no omniscient God.

With regard to all such arguments, of course, we will want to consider possible replies. Such is the work of the following sections.

Another application of the basic Cantorian argument—not too surprising, perhaps, given the work throughout—is against any approach to possible worlds in terms of maximal sets of propositions.

As noted in chapter one, such an approach appears explicitly in the work of Robert M. Adams. In Adams' outline, it will be remembered, possible worlds are given a contextual analysis in terms of world stories, themselves defined as maximal consistent sets of propositions (Adams 1974).

Plantinga's outline, though phrased in terms of states of affairs, is very similar:

Now a possible world is a possible state of affairs. But not just any possible state of affairs is a possible world; to achieve this distinction, a state of affairs must be *complete* or *maximal*. We may explain this as follows. Let us say that a state of affairs S *includes* a state of affairs $S*$ if it is not possible that S obtain and $S*$ fail to obtain; and let us say that S *precludes* $S*$ if it is not possible that both obtain. A maximal state of affairs, then, is one that for every state of affairs S, either includes or precludes S. And a possible world is a state of affairs that is both possible and maximal.

The set of propositions true in a given world W is the *book* on W. Books, like worlds, have a maximality property: for any proposition p and book B, either B contains p or B contains $\bar{p}$, the denial of p. The book on α, the actual world, is the set of all true propositions. (Plantinga 1976, 258–259)[11]

On any such account, the actual world will be the maximal consistent set of propositions that actually obtain—a maximal and consistent set of all and only truths—or at least an appropriately fleshed out correlate to such a set. By the argument with which I began, however, there is not and cannot be any set of all truths. *Any* set of true propositions will leave some proposition out, and thus there can be no maximal set of truths. In the sense of 'actual world' crucial to an approach such as Adams' and Plantinga's, then, there is and can be no actual world.

The argument can also, of course, be extended against the existence of *possible* worlds on any such approach. Let us identify possible worlds with maximal consistent sets of propositions, and let T^w be the maximal consistent set of all propositions true in world w. In a simple form of the argument, one can point out that there will be a necessary truth for each element of $\mathscr{P}T^w$ and that necessary truths will hold in all possible worlds.[12] Using the basic strategy for introducing contingent propositions outlined above, one might alternatively envisage a distinct contingent proposition true in w corresponding to each element of $\mathscr{P}T^w$. In either case, however, there will be more truths that hold in w—or more propositions that would have been true had w been actual—than are included in T^w. There can, for no world, be a set of *all* truths that hold in that world. If possible worlds are to be identified with maximal consistent sets of propositions, there simply can be no possible worlds. The basic lesson of the Cantorian argument here seems to be that a maximality requirement on possible worlds of the sort at issue simply cannot logically be fulfilled.[13]

In the sections that follow, I want to consider a number of possible replies.

3   Alternative Set Theories: A Possible Way Out?

This much, at least, seems to be a solid result of the work above: there can be no set of all truths. Moreover, the implications of that result seem to extend to epistemology and philosophy of religion on the one hand and to metaphysics on the other: there can be no set of things an omniscient being would have to know, for example, nor can there be either world stories or worlds construed in terms of maximal sets of propositions.

The fact that the notion of *sets* plays such a central role in the argument may seem to promise a convenient way out, however. For even if there can be no *set* of all truths, it might be proposed, there might be a *nonset something else* of all truths. Though maximal sets of propositions or of what an omniscient being would have to know seem to lead to logical difficulties, perhaps there might be a nonset something else appropriate to the propositions of a world or the knowledge of an omniscient mind.

Despite the argument above, then, might there not be a nonset something else of all truths or of all propositions? The short answer, I think, is no. A full answer demands a look at some of the details of standard and alternative set theories.

Within naive set theory one all too quickly encounters the contradictions of Cantor's paradox regarding a set of all sets and Russell's paradox regarding a set of all sets not members of themselves. Cantor's theorem states that every set will be smaller than its power set: $z < \{x \mid x \subseteq z\}$. Cantor's *paradox* arises when the set of all sets, V, is substituted here for z, which gives us the impossible result that such a set must be smaller than itself. Russell's paradox arises when we suppose a set of all sets not members of themselves, $\{u \mid u \notin u\}$, and derive a contradiction from the supposition that it either is or is not a member of itself.

All axiomatic set theory, standard or alternative, is essentially a response to these two paradoxes. With regard to Cantor's paradox in particular, the basic strategy is either to deny admission to V or the like or to cripple mechanisms of proof necessary for relevant forms of Cantor's theorem.

Let us start with what alternative set theories are alternatives to: standard Zermelo-Fraenkel (ZF) set theory. The contradictions of Russell's and Cantor's paradoxes are avoided within ZF by replacing an unrestricted principle of comprehension often attributed to Cantor,[14]

$$\exists S \forall x(x \in S \equiv Fx),$$

where F can be any condition, with the restricted *Aussonderung* axiom,

$$\exists S \forall x(x \in S \equiv x \in A \mathbin{\&} Fx),$$

where A is any set. Given this replacement, there simply *are* no sets such as Cantor and Russell envisage.

The spirit of the argument in sections 1 and 2 above, in effect, is that a 'set of all truths' leads to similar difficulties and must similarly be abandoned: there simply is no such set.

With an eye to the distinction between pure set theory and the richer theories of philosophical importance here, I might put the matter as follows. The contradictions of Cantor's and Russell's paradoxes quickly arise for even a pure naive theory in which there are no elements other than sets. The standard response of pure ZF is to restrict comprehension for sets of sets; there can, for example, be no set of *all* sets.

Here, of course, what is at issue is an ontology richer than that of pure set theory: it is not merely sets that are at issue but truths as well, for example. Given very basic intuitions regarding sets and truths, however, it appears that a notion of a set of all truths leads to difficulties very much like those familiar from a naive theory purely of sets. I have in effect argued above that the appropriate response here is also the same: to opt for a more sophisticated theory in which there are major restrictions on sets of *truths*, a ZF-like theory in which there is, in particular, no set of *all* truths.

Within ZF, of course, sets are all the classes there are. For ZF, 'set' and 'class' are mere synonyms, and so, of course, in any ZF-like theory there will be no class of all truths either. There are also alternative responses to Cantor's and Russell's paradoxes, however, embodied in alternative systems of set theory. In some of these something like Cantor's and Russell's sets do appear, though in the guise of a nonset something else, in the guise of a "class" or "proper class" or "ultimate class," carefully distinguished from sets and for which different principles will hold.

In what follows, I want to consider several important alternative set theories: those of Quine's "New Foundations" (NF) and *Mathematical*

Logic (ML), von Neumann–Bernays (VNB), Kelley-Morse (KM), and Ackerman (A).[15] For my purposes, of course, ultimately at issue are theories of these basic forms but with ontologies rich enough to include truths and propositions.

With the introductory exception of NF, the central strategy of each of these systems is to escape set-theoretic paradoxes by supplementing sets with an additional category of nonset classes. But the basic framework of none, I want to argue, ultimately offers any hope, except at quite unacceptable cost, for even a *class* of all truths. In section 4, I will go on to consider a very different kind of alternative theory; one that offers us not *more* than standard set theory, as these do, but significantly less.

Let us start, then, with NF. Quine's "New Foundations" contains merely an axiom of extensionality and the axiom schema

$$\exists y \forall x \, (x \in y \equiv Fx),$$

but strictly subject to a provision of *stratification*: that within condition F there always be a way of flanking '$\in$' with consecutive, ascending indices.

Russell's 'set of all sets not members of themselves' does not appear in NF precisely because of the stratification requirement. But Cantor's universal set *does*, and appears moreover fully as a *set V*.

What then of Cantor's paradox? Within ZF, contradiction in this regard is avoided by eliminating V. Within NF, in contrast, contradiction is avoided by crippling the basic mechanism of the argument crucial to Cantor's paradox: '$z < \{x \mid x \subseteq z\}$' is simply not provable for all sets. It is not provable, in particular, for *non-Cantorian* sets within NF, which have the anomalous feature of containing more elements than their singleton subsets, in Quine's notation, the feature that $\iota``z < z$. V, among others, is a non-Cantorian set within NF.

Despite anomalies, the basic structure of NF might seem to offer a promising way out for a set of all *truths*. The difficulties posed in preceding sections, after all, do rely on a basic Cantorian argument, and within NF the basic mechanism of that argument has been disarmed. Consider, then, a form of NF expanded to encompass truths as well as pure sets; might not this offer an alternative set theory in which a place *could* be found for a set of all truths?

Unfortunately, any adoption of an NF-like theory to save a "set of all truths" proves to be a very desperate move. For the costs of NF turn out to be enormous.

Rosser and Wang (1950) initially showed that no model of NF, no inter-pretation of '∈' compatible with the axioms, could make well-orderings of both the lesser-to-greater relation among ordinals and that among finite cardinals except by interpreting '=' as something other than identity. Specker (1953) went on to show that the non-Cantorian sets of NF cause the relations of lesser to greater among cardinals to fail to be a well-ordering, and he thereby a produced a disproof of the axiom of choice within NF.[16] Finally, and perhaps most crucially, mathematical induction fails within NF for unstratified conditions. As Quine concludes,

The fact remains that mathematical induction of unstratified conditions is not generally provided for in NF. This omission seems needless and arbitrary. It hints that the standards of class existence in NF approximate insufficiently, after all, to the considerations that are really central to the paradoxes and their avoidance. (Quine 1969, 294–299; see also Bar-Hillel 1967)

Any NF-like theory expanded to include truths or propositions can, of course, be expected to inherit the critical difficulties of NF proper.

It was precisely in response to these difficulties that Quine proposed the system of *Mathematical Logic*. ML is basically an enlargement of NF so as to include a category of *ultimate classes* in addition to sets.[17] To call x a *set* within ML is to say that it is a member of something, that $\exists z(x \in z)$. *Classes*, in contrast, spring up for every membership condition without restriction, taking as members all sets meeting that condition:

$$\exists y \forall x(x \in y \equiv \exists z(x \in z) \ \& \ Fx)$$

With both classes and sets on hand in ML it is important to distinguish between V, a "genuine universe" that includes all classes, and $\bigcup V$, which includes merely all sets. Correspondingly, it becomes important to distin-guish between $\{x \mid Fx\}$, which consists of all classes meeting a condition F, and $\hat{x}Fx$, a class merely of all sets meeting that condition.

The axiom of extensionality is, of course, retained from NF. What were the comprehension axioms of NF, however, complete with their stratifica-tion requirement, are transformed into mere *sethood* axioms for ML. A wholly new and unrestricted comprehension schema,

$\hat{u}Fu \in V$,

allows us to include ultimate classes in addition to sets.

The benefits of ML, at least as a pure theory of sets and classes, are many. NF's inadequacies with regard to mathematical induction are now remedied. What were non-Cantorian sets in NF, though preserved in ML, are transformed into fully Cantorian classes by a subtle change in the definition of '≤'—$\forall z(z \leq \iota"z)$ will hold in the sense of '≤' outlined for ML—and thus become much less anomalous. The axiom of choice, in at least a slightly weakened form, can now be restored.[18]

ML has a category of ultimate classes beyond mere sets, of course. Does that mean that a form of ML expanded to include truths as well as sets might offer room for an ultimate class of all *truths*? Things don't turn out to be that easy.

Consider first the Russell and Cantor problems within a pure ML confined to pure sets and classes. Here we might be content to take Russell's set as $\hat{u}(u \notin u)$. If so, paradox is at least temporarily avoided; within ML both $\hat{u}(u \notin u)$ and $\hat{u}(u = u)$ do have a perfectly respectable place provided by the unrestricted principle of comprehension for classes. But what that principle gives us in each case is, of course, a *class* all members of which are merely *sets*.[19]

What then of a class of all classes $\{u \mid u = u\}$ or a class of all non-self-membered classes $\{u \mid u \notin u\}$? In contrast to $\hat{u}(u \notin u)$ and $\hat{u}(u = u)$, each of these *would* qualify as a class of classes. But classes composed of classes beyond mere sets are not provided for within ML. In the form $\{u \mid u \notin u\}$, Russell's class simply does not exist. With regard to a Cantorian class of all classes $V = \{u \mid u = u\}$, Quine notes, "ML escapes paradox not as NF did, by a breakdown in the proof of '$z < \{x \mid x \subseteq z\}$', but as Zermelo's system did: by not having V" (Quine 1969, 308).

What then are the prospects for a set or a class of all *truths* within an ML-like system? Consider first a variant on ML in which we admit truths "at the bottom," as it were, as ur-elements suitable for set membership. To change ML as little as possible in the process, let us leave stratification requirements on sets of sets as they stand, and continue to admit classes only of sets. We will thus not provide, at this point, for classes of truths. On the other hand, let us leave *sets* of truths unrestricted: for any condition C, there will be a set of those truths satisfying C.

Within such a modification of ML, can we contemplate a *set* of all truths? No. For suppose any set of all truths T within such a system, and consider all subsets of T. For each of these there will be a truth. By a Cantorian argument of now familiar form, here by the fact that truths satisfying any condition will form a set, there will be more subsets of T, and hence more truths, than T contains. There can then be no set of all truths.[20]

Can ML be modified so as to admit a *class* of all truths? In modifying ML so as to countenance classes of truths, we will presumably retain an unrestricted comprehension principle for classes, though now rewritten to handle classes of truths as well as classes of sets.[21] The least disruptive way to make such a modification is perhaps simply to add the following principle:

PRINCIPLE OF UNRESTRICTED COMPREHENSION FOR CLASSES OF TRUTHS   There is a class C of precisely those truths t satisfying condition $C(t)$, where $C(t)$ is any condition.

Would this give us a way of introducing a class of all truths within the basic structure of an ML-like system? The answer is again a definitive no. For suppose there *were* a class of all truths T within such a system, as unrestricted comprehension would seem to suggest, and consider the subclasses of T. Each such subclass consists purely of truths and is thus provided for by the principle of comprehension. For each such subclass, however, there will also be a truth: that it is a class, for example, or that it contains the members it does. By an argument of standard Cantorian form, fully applicable here, there will thus be more truths than contained in T.[22] T cannot be a class of *all* truths, on pain of contradiction, and any principle of comprehension that forced us to admit a class of all truths would simply render an ML-like system inconsistent.[23] So though ML, taken as a pure theory of sets, does compensate for some of the glaring inadequacies of NF, ML-like theories do not seem to offer any real place for either a set or a class of all truths.

ML, as noted, is an expansion of NF that incorporates ultimate classes. The von Neumann–Bernays system can be thought of as a similar expansion of ZF that includes ultimate classes. *Sets* within VNB, as within ML, are classes that are members of further classes. Ultimate classes are not. Alternatively, sets are those classes *smaller* than something:

$$\exists y(x \in y) \equiv \exists y(x < y)$$

Ultimate classes are those equinumerous with a class of all sets $\bigcup V$.

The major difference between ML and VNB, beyond differences between the systems NF and ZF on which they are built, is the following. ML contains an unrestricted axiom of comprehension for classes: a class of all sets satisfying C is admitted for any condition C. Within VNB the classes provided for are likewise limited to classes of sets, but comprehension for classes is further limited to *predicative* cases. All bound variables of conditions C are restricted to sets:

PRINCIPLE OF PREDICATIVE COMPREHENSION FOR CLASSES   There is a class C that consists of precisely those sets x that satisfy the condition $C(x)$, where $C(x)$ is a condition that does not contain quantifiers over classes, i.e., $C(x)$ does not contain expressions of the form 'for every class X' or 'there exists a class X'.[24]

Within VNB as within ZF, which it incorporates, there can of course be no set of all sets, nor any set of all non-self-membered sets. Within a VNB-like system modified minimally to include sets of *truths*, introduced along the lines of sets of sets within pure VNB, there similarly can be no set of all truths, for standard reasons.

In VNB, as in ML, however, there *can* be a *class* of all sets, and there *can* be a *class* of all non-self-membered sets. It is crucial that these remain classes whose the members are mere sets. Within VNB, as within ML, no classes of *classes* are provided for at all. VNB offers no place for a class of non-self-membered classes, then, and similarly gives us no class of all classes.

What, then, of prospects for a class of all *truths*? Here as before, the natural way of extending VNB to admit classes of truths, it seems, would be to follow the pattern laid down for classes of sets within the basic theory. As before, let us thus admit a class C of those truths satisfying a condition $C(t)$ only where $C(t)$ is a predicative condition:

PRINCIPLE OF PREDICATIVE COMPREHENSION FOR CLASSES OF TRUTHS   There is a class C that consists of precisely those truths t that satisfy a condition $C(t)$, where $C(t)$ does not contain quantifiers over classes.

What makes this a promising move is the following. In pure VNB, unlike in pure ML, Cantor's theorem is not provable for classes: it can't be shown that every class will be smaller than the class of all its subclasses (in Quine's symbolism, $z < \{x \mid x \subseteq z\}$).[25] Within VNB the "diagonal" element crucial for such a proof—an element specified as including all classes that are not elements of their assigned class $f(c)$ for a chosen function f—is simply not guaranteed to exist as a class. In particular, because of $f(c)$, the defining condition for such a diagonal element may fail to satisfy the predicativity requirements of VNB. The fact that the basic mechanism of such an argument is crippled, then, might seem to offer hope for a class of all truths within a VNB-like system.

Consider how at least one form of the Cantorian argument against a class of all truths would break down here. We start by supposing a class T of all truths and consider its subclasses. Can there be a one-to-one mapping of elements of T onto subclasses of T? No, the standard argument goes, for consider any proposed mapping f and the class C^* of all elements t of T that are not members of the subclass $f(t)$ onto which they are mapped. Since no element of t can be mapped onto C^*, so the argument goes, the class of subclasses of T must be larger than T itself. The same will hold for a class of truths constructed by introducing a distinct truth for each member of the power class. Thus T cannot be a class of *all* truths.

The crucial assumption here that a class C^* *exists*, however, will not be assured within a VNB-like system. In particular, the mapping function $f(t)$, and thus the defining condition for C^* may be *im*predicative in form and thus fail to guarantee a class. The argument doesn't go through, and (in this form, at least) the Cantorian threat to a class of all truths is disarmed.[26]

Any hope this might seem to offer for a class of all truths proves to be short-lived, however. For here, as in the case of NF, the costs of seriously adopting something like VNB turn out to be exorbitantly high. Moreover, here, as in the case of NF, a major cost is again a sacrifice of mathematical induction. As Lévy notes, drawing on work by Mostowski,

A particularly embarrassing fact about VNB is that in VNB ... one cannot prove all instances of the induction schema, "If 0 fulfills the condition $D(x)$ and for every natural number n, if n fulfills $D(x)$ then $n + 1$ fulfills $D(x)$ too, then every number fulfills $D(x)$." (Fraenkel, Bar-Hillel, and Lévy 1973, 39; the original work appears in Mostowski 1950)

The parallel between the sorrows of NF and the sorrows of VNB is in fact quite close. In both cases Cantorian argument is blocked—in NF, Cantorian argument regarding sets; in VNB, Cantorian argument regarding classes—but only at the cost in each case of crippling corresponding forms of mathematical induction as well.

Here we might try to follow the example that Quine sets in moving from NF to ML. ML, it will be remembered, avoided the difficulties of induction that plagued NF by including a principle of unrestricted comprehension for classes. Can we similarly modify VNB to free comprehension for impredicative cases? Suppose we replace predicative comprehension for classes with the following:

PRINCIPLE OF IMPREDICATIVE COMPREHENSION FOR CLASSES   There is a class
C that consists of precisely those sets x that satisfy condition $C(x)$, where
$C(x)$ is *any* condition.

What this essentially gives us is Kelley-Morse set theory.[27] Pure KM
does indeed have advantages over VNB similar to the advantages of ML
over NF. Impredicative comprehension, of course, allows for the existence
of classes that predicative comprehension does not, and thus the classes of
KM are a significant enlargement over those of VNB. One can, moreover,
prove infinitely many statements about only sets within KM that one
cannot in VNB. Finally, in KM, unlike in VNB, all instances of the
induction schema will be provable (see Lévy 1976, 197 ff.).

Despite these important features, however, it turns out that KM-like
theories don't ultimately offer any greater hope for a set or class of all
truths than do the alternative theories considered above.

KM, which can be seen as a variant of VNB, is still built essentially on
the foundation of ZF. Within KM, as within ZF, there can be neither a set
of all sets nor a set of all non-self-membered sets. Within a KM-like system
modified to include sets of truths along the lines of sets of sets within pure
KM, there will similarly be no set of all truths.

Within KM, as within ML and VNB, there *is a class* of all sets, and there
is a class of all non-self-membered sets. But here, as there, classes of *classes*
are not provided for. Within KM, as within its predecessors, then, we are
given neither a class of all classes nor a class of all non-self-membered
classes.

What of the possibility of a class of all *truths* within a KM-like system?
Much of the power of KM stems from the crucial feature it shares with
ML: an unrestricted comprehension principle for classes. In the case of
ML-like systems, however, it was precisely the *un*restricted character of
comprehension that seemed to doom any class of all truths. Much the same
story holds for KM.

Here as before, the natural course seems to be to expand KM to a
KM-like system incorporating classes of truths by introducing a correspondingly unrestricted comprehension principle for classes of truths.
Given such a principle, however, the basic Cantorian argument against a
class of all truths offered in the case of ML can simply be repeated. Given
any supposed set T of all truths, we will be able to show that there are more
truths than elements of T. If the principle of comprehension forces us to

admit a class of all truths, it will be sufficient to render any KM-like system inconsistent.

The lesson of alternative set theories considered so far—NF, ML, VNB, and KM—seems to be uncompromisingly negative regarding prospects for any collection of all truths. Stratified and predicative comprehension principles, as in NF and VNB, do seem to cripple the basic Cantorian argument at issue, and in that sense they do seem to offer a tantalizing prospect for some global class of all truths. But in both cases the cost of such restricted comprehension seems to be a corresponding and strongly counterintuitive crippling of mathematical induction as well. Such a limitation, as Quine notes, seems "needless and arbitrary" (Quine 1969, 299).

The alternative seems to be an *un*restricted principle of comprehension on the pattern of comprehension for classes within ML and KM. Expanded to classes of *truths*, however, such a principle gives us a full-blown Cantorian argument against a class of all truths and a none too subtle threat of inconsistency as a result.

Here let me finally mention an intriguing variation offered by Ackerman set theory, notable for a number of elegant features, though perhaps not ultimately offering any greater hope for a set or class of all truths.

Within A, as a pure system, we are given a universe of objects and a membership relation $\in$. Two objects are identical just in case they have the same members, and thus it seems natural to think of such objects as classes.

Some classes C, but not all, fall under a primitive predicate $M(C)$, which in turn seems quite naturally interpreted as 'C is a set.'[28] In pure form the variables X, Y, ... of A range over classes, but additional set variables x, y, ... can be introduced as abbreviatory devices for $\forall X(M(X) \rightarrow \ldots)$, $\forall Y(M(Y) \rightarrow \ldots)$, and the like. A is thus a "class-down" theory, in a sense, rather than "set-up"; within A we have sets as classes for which the primitive $M(C)$ holds, rather than classes introduced as additional entities "on top of" sets.

The theory employs a familiar impredicative comprehension principle for classes:

PRINCIPLE OF IMPREDICATIVE COMPREHENSION   There exists a class C that contains precisely those sets x that satisfy the condition $C(x)$, where $C(x)$ is any condition.

Principles for sets, on the other hand, are as follows:

PRINCIPLE OF HEREDITY   If Y is a member of a set x, then Y is a set too: $Y \in x \rightarrow M(Y)$.

PRINCIPLE OF SUBSETS   If Y is a subclass of a set x, then Y is a set too: $Y \subseteq x \rightarrow M(Y)$.

PRINCIPLE OF COMPREHENSION FOR SETS   If the only classes X that satisfy the condition $C(X)$ are sets, then there exists a set w that consists exactly of those sets that satisfy $C(X)$, where $C(X)$ is any condition that does not involve the predicate M and has no parameters other than set parameters:

$$\forall x_1 \forall x_2 \ldots \forall x_n [\forall X(C(X) \rightarrow M(X)) \rightarrow \exists w \forall X(X \in w \equiv C(X))],$$

where $C(X)$ does not involve M and has no parameters other than x_1, $x_2, \ldots x_n$.

With additional axioms of extensionality and foundation, these give us a system with a number of interesting features. Despite its top-down character, for example, A turns out to have a very pretty correspondence with ZF. Every statement of ZF is a statement of A.[29] Those statements of ZF provable in A turn out to be precisely the theorems of ZF. It can further be shown that A is consistent if and only if ZF is (Lévy 1976, 211). It also turns out, interestingly enough, that if A is consistent, there can be no expression $D(X)$ of A that contains no parameters other than set parameters, doesn't involve the predicate $M(X)$, and yet is equivalent to $M(X)$. If A is consistent, in other words, the notion of sethood expressed by the primitive $M(X)$ is essentially expressible *only* by means of that primitive (Lévy 1976, 209).

Of course, here as in all set theories, it is the comprehension principles that are crucial to the paradoxes and related Cantorian arguments. Both restrictions on the comprehension principle for sets above are necessary to avoid the standard paradoxes. Were we to lift the restriction that $C(X)$ not involve the sethood primitive $M(X)$, we could use $(M(X) \& C'(X))$ as $C(X)$, with the result that the class $\{X \mid C'(X)\}$ would be a set for any condition $C'(X)$. Among others, this would admit the class $\{x \mid x \notin x\}$ as a set, which lands us immediately in the contradictions of Russell's paradox. It is also necessary that $C(X)$ be restricted to set parameters in set comprehension. Otherwise, we could choose the condition $X \in Y$ for $C(X)$, with the result that for any class Y, if all members of Y are sets, then the class $\{x \mid x \in Y\}$ must also be a set. Using the class $\{x \mid C(x)\}$ for Y, where C is any condition, we would then get the result that every class $\{x \mid C(x)\}$ is a set, which once again leads straight to Russell's paradox. Within A, as within class theories in general, the collection of all sets V and of all non-self-membered sets *can* appear, but only as classes rather than as sets.

Within A, as within its predecessors, Russellian and Cantorian difficulties regarding *classes* are blocked by limiting class comprehension to classes of *sets*. Were we to broaden A's unrestricted comprehension to classes of *classes*, we would again face the standard difficulties in the standard ways.

What, then, of a set or class of all *truths* within an A-like system? Here as elsewhere the basic framework seems incapable of admitting all truths as either a set or a class.

To begin with, there can be no *set* of all truths. All theorems of ZF regarding sets, I have noted, appear again within A—that is indeed part of its beauty. In an A-like system in which sets of truths are admitted on the same pattern as sets of sets within pure A, we will then get the same result as in a ZF-like system: there can be no set of *all* truths.

Any *class* of all truths proves equally problematic. Within A, as within KM and ML, we have a principle of impredicative comprehension for classes. If we modify A to admit classes of *truths* on the same pattern, the results outlined for KM and ML above return to haunt us: we get both a full Cantorian argument against a class of all truths and an immediate threat of inconsistency.

None of the alternative set theories surveyed, then, seems to offer any very promising route of escape. The technical problem that has dogged our steps throughout is basically this. An *un*restricted principle of comprehension for classes—such as that in KM, ML, or A—if extended to give us classes of truths, allows too much of the basic mechanism of a Cantorian argument to permit any hope for a class of *all* truths. Comprehension restricted to stratified or predicative conditions, on the other hand, such as in NF and VNB, *does* seem to promise the possibility of a class or set of all truths precisely because it cripples the basic mechanism of the Cantorian argument. But in each case the Cantorian argument is crippled only at the cost of seriously crippling mathematical induction as well.[30]

Even more serious than that central technical difficulty, however, is a deep *intuitive* problem for the alternative set theories considered. The basic strategy of alternative theories throughout has been an appeal to some type of collection *beyond* sets, in particular, an appeal to ultimate or proper classes. The very notion of ultimate or proper classes, moreover, in whatever system, is the notion of classes that will escape paradox precisely because they themselves will not be members of further classes.[31]

A class of all truths, however, would not appear to qualify as appropriately ultimate in that sense. Wouldn't such a class be a member of the class of classes of propositions? Of the class of classes containing one or more truths?

With an eye to the issue of omniscience, consider also the class of classes of things known by existent beings. Wouldn't what God knows be a member of *that* class?

Possible worlds and world stories seem, if anything, *less* amenable to treatment as proper or ultimate classes. For consider the class of worlds in which I exist and the class of worlds in which this vase is hit with a hammer. Current philosophical use quite generally seems to demand *classes* of possible worlds.

In the end, I think, the ultimate classes of alternative set theories do not turn out even intuitively to be a very promising option. This last difficulty is closely related to Quine's general objection: "[VNB modified] shares a serious drawback with ML, and with von Neumann's unextended system, and with any other system that invokes ultimate classes.... We want to be able to form finite classes, in all ways, of all things there are assumed to be ..., and the trouble is that ultimate classes will not belong" (Quine 1969, 321).[32]

The alternative set theories considered above, however, have essentially been *class* theories: attempts to supplement set theory with the addition of suitably specified classes. In the next section I want to consider a very different proposal for saving the notion of a set of all truths and the like: not by *adding* something to standard set theory but by taking something away.

4   The Problem without Power Sets

Christopher Menzel has proposed saving the notion of a set of all truths and the like not by an *amplification* of standard set theory but by a significant *amputation*, in particular, an amputation of the power set axiom.[33]

VNB and similar class theories, Menzel argues, here in accord with my conclusions above, do not offer any significant hope for either a set or class of all truths, nor for possible worlds construed in terms of world stories, maximal consistent sets of propositions.[34] But standard ZF set theory minus the power set axiom, he suggests, *does* offer such a possibility.

Perhaps the world story theorist, Menzel suggests, though clearly a profligate realist with regard to the existence of propositions, can follow an abstemious constructivist line when it comes to sets:

> By adopting ZF − Power (or some similarly conservative set theory), then, and adjusting it appropriately to allow for the existence of large sets (and urelements),[35] the world-story theorist is free to postulate the existence of his world-stories without fear of paradox, at least by way of [the Cantorian] argument; for that argument depends essentially on there being a power set of the world-story S; but there is simply no way of generating the full classical power set of an infinite set in ZF − Power. (Menzel 1986b, 71).

The promise of such a proposal is clear. The Cantorian argument against a set of all truths with which we began, for example, relies quite explicitly on a particular power set: 'For suppose there *is* a set T, and consider its power set, containing all subsets of T.' Menzel's strategy is to eliminate precisely that feature of standard set theory, the power set axiom, that assures us of the existence of that further set. We might also put the issue as follows. In section 3 the only hope that seemed to appear for a set or class of all truths was within those systems that crippled the basic Cantorian argument. Menzel's amputation of the power set axiom is perhaps the most direct crippling possible.

In the end, however, large sets within ZF − power don't seem to prove any more satisfactory for a set of all truths or the like than did the ultimate classes considered in section 3.

Not too surprisingly, sacrifice of the power set axiom results in quite major technical limitations; at one blow we are effectively exiled from Cantor's paradise.[36] It is far from clear, moreover, that ZF − power applied as Menzel envisages would really satisfy any constructivist scruples. Menzel relies on the fact that "there is simply no way of generating the full classical power set of an infinite set in ZF − Power." But, of course, there is no way of *generating* basic infinite sets within ZF − power at all; all such sets must be added by fiat in terms of special axioms. The set of zero and its successors appears by axiom within ZF, and a set of all ordinals is added by a special axiom in the system Menzel proposes in 1986a/b. If we are to include the reals, world stories of infinitely many propositions, and infinite sets of world stories within ZF − power, we will need special axiomatic provision for these as well—a prodigal postulation of sets far from constructivist in spirit.

But for present purposes the most telling objection against ZF − power is simply that it doesn't ultimately avoid the central Cantorian difficutlies for which Menzel invokes it. It turns out that because a set of all truths (or the like) is at issue, sacrifice of even the power set axiom is not enough.

For consider the following argument:[37] Let us suppose we *did* have a set T of all truths in an expanded system with the basic structure of ZF − power. Then by the axiom schema of separation, adapted directly from ZF, we would have as a subset of T a set of all truths satisfying a particular condition $B(x)$.[38] As long as the basic language is rich enough to express the notion that a truth t is about a topic c, it appears, one such condition will be 'x is about a set of truths'. By separation, then, we would have a set C of all truths about sets of truths.

More formally, using 'Axy' to indicate that x is about y, the condition 'x is about a set of truths' is

$$\exists y \forall z (z \in y \rightarrow z \in T . \& \ Axy).$$

The axiom schema of separation, taken directly from ZF, is

$$\forall z_1 \ldots \forall z_n \forall a \forall y \forall x (x \in y \equiv x \in a \ \& \ B(x)),$$

where $z_1, \ldots, z_n$ are the free variables of $B(x)$ other than x and the only restriction on $B(x)$ is that it does not contain y as a free variable.[39] Using T for a in this schema and the condition above for $B(x)$ gives us a set C of all truths about sets of truths:

$$\forall x (x \in C \equiv x \in T \ \& \ \exists y \forall z (z \in y \rightarrow z \in T . \& \ Axy)).$$

The existence of a set C, however, leads to a reductio. In particular, C would be larger than T. For consider any one-to-one function f from T into C mapping truths onto truths concerning sets of truths, and consider further a set C' of all truths that do not belong to the sets their assigned element is about. If we use '$a(f(x))$' to indicate the set (or union of sets) $f(x)$ is about,

$$\forall x (x \in C' \equiv x \in T \ \& \ x \notin a(f(x))).$$

Clearly, C will contain some truth about C', just as it contains some truth regarding any set of truths. But by familiar reasoning, f can assign no element of t to any truth about C'. C is larger than T. One form of the reductio, then, is this: given a set T of all truths, there would be a subset C larger than the set T of which it is a subset.[40]

The reductio can also take another form. Since each element of C is a truth, there are more truths than elements of T: T cannot, as assumed, be a set of *all* truths. A similar argument would, of course, apply to world stories as well.

So, in order to escape the Cantorian difficulties facing a set of all truths, or a set of all propositions or of all propositions true in a given possible world, even heroic sacrifice of the power set axiom proves insufficient. In particular, to escape the difficulties posed in terms of C above, something *more* would have to be sacrificed.

Here one *might* go on to impose still tighter restrictions on the axiom schema of separation. One might, for example, insist on a system whose language excludes or severely restricts the notion of truths about sets of truths. Since there clearly is a truth about any set of truths, however, this would seem far from satisfactory. Such measures have an air of extremity and desperation and would at best promise a "set" or "collection" of all truths or the like only in a sense of 'set' or 'collection' so thin as to be intuitively unrecognizable and philosophically uninteresting. Here, as elsewhere, perhaps we should simply concede that there can be no set of all truths.

The real lesson of this extended discussion of alternative set theories, I think, is that the fundamental conceptual difficulties at issue have a basic intuitive force and an intuitive variety of forms that are not going to be avoided merely by the introduction of some new formalism. The problems at issue don't appear to be merely surface features of some unfortunate symbolism. They seem rather to be difficulties embedded in our notions of truths, propositions, possibilities, and totalities themselves—difficulties that any system that adequately captures such notions will have to reflect, and that no simple appeal to alternative systems is going to dispel.

5   The Appeal to Quantification

One application of the Cantorian argument, we've seen, is against possible worlds construed in terms of maximal consistent sets of propositions. The truth of the matter, it appears, is that there simply cannot *be* any such maximal set; for any set of propositions true at any world w, there will be some propositions true at w that the set will leave out.

Yet possible worlds have not always been outlined in terms of *sets*, even by those sympathetic to an understanding of possible worlds in terms of propositions. A variant approach, one that seems at least initially less vulnerable to Cantorian argument, is to offer a quantificational outline instead.

The outline Plantinga offers at one point is the following:

> Let us say that a state of affairs *S* *includes* a state of affairs *S′* if it is not possible (in the broadly logical sense) that *S* obtain and *S′* fail to obtain, ... a state of affairs *S* *precludes* *S′* if it is not possible that both obtain.... A state of affairs *S* is *complete* or *maximal* if for every state of affairs *S′*, *S* includes *S′* or precludes *S′*. And a possible world is simply a possible state of affairs that is maximal. (Plantinga 1974, 45)[41]

Here it is not the phrase 'state of affairs' that is of importance; states of affairs don't appear to offer any particular advantages in the present context that propositions do not, and a Cantorian argument is as easily constructible against maximal sets of states of affairs as against maximal sets of propositions.

Rather, what is important is the quantificational form of Plantinga's outline. Rewritten in terms of world stories and propositions, such an outline might read as follows:

W is a possible world story iff for all propositions *p*, *W* entails *p* or *W* entails $\sim p$.

Here sets don't appear explicitly at all. In fact, in this formulation, unlike the passage quoted from Plantinga above, even the set-suggestive notion of inclusion is avoided.[42]

What such an account seems to suggest is that perhaps we can do *without* sets or classes, and thereby avoid the difficulties we have seen to plague them, simply by relying on quantification instead. There is, we might admit, no set, no class, no collection, and no totality of all truths; all of these seem openly vulnerable to Cantorian argument. But it might appear that we could nevertheless speak of *all* truths simply by using something like the following quantificational form:

$$\forall p(Tp \to \ldots p \ldots)$$

There is similarly, we might admit, no set, no class, no collection, and no totality of all that an omniscient being would have to know. But it might appear that we could nonetheless define a coherent notion of omniscience in purely quantificational terms:

A being x is *omniscient* $=_{df}$ for all p, p is true iff x believes that p AND x believes that p iff x knows that p.

Or slightly more formally, with 'Bxp' for 'x believes that p' and 'Kxp' for 'x knows that p',

A being x is *omniscient* $=_{df} \forall p(Tp \equiv Bxp$.&. $Bxp \equiv Kxp)$.[43]

We might similarly admit that there is no set, class, or collection of all propositions true in our world or in any other possible world. In that sense both our universe and others fail to form complete totalities. But it might appear that we could nonetheless speak quantificationally of all propositions true in a possible world w as follows:

$\forall p(p$ is true in $w \rightarrow \ldots p \ldots)$

Does a direct appeal to quantification offer a way out? Despite its initial attractiveness, any such account will face a number of challenging difficulties.

One at least apparent difficulty is this. All of the outlines above rely on universal propositional quantification. But the only formal semantics for quantification we have is in terms of *sets*, and thus the only formal semantics we have for propositional quantification is in terms of a set of all propositions. Isn't it thus the case that the 'set of all propositions' that we try to avoid by appeal to quantification simply reappears in our formal semantics?

How serious such a difficulty really is depends, I think, on what we expect of formal semantics. If formal semantics is thought of as an attempt to explicate the meaning of our symbolism or to indicate how that symbolism is to be understood, this does indeed seem a major difficulty. For in that case the only formal understanding of quantification we have would seem to reintroduce precisely the global sets that appeal to quantification was meant to avoid. One way of reading the results of section 3 above is, of course, that no alternative formal semantics in terms of classes would fare any better in this regard.

But if formal semantics is viewed as something significantly weaker, perhaps as the mere construction of formal models of *some* features of our symbolism, adequate for *some* purposes, this difficulty may not be so telling. Here it will still be the case that no formal semantics we can offer, short of reintroducing a 'set of all propositions' or the like, can capture both the intended scope of our quantifiers and a genuine application to propositions. In that regard we will lack a formal model. But what we will lack, it might be said, is *merely* a formal model. Formal modeling in general may offer a poor shadow of either the meaning of our symbolism or our understanding of it, and thus the failure of such formal modeling for quantification need not reflect any failure in our general understanding of its meaning.

At any rate, here I want to consider the purer form of an appeal to quantification: the proposal that we should simply use raw quantification *without* any formal semantics. Suppose that we not only concede that there is no set, class, or totality of all truths or all propositions but at the same time abandon any standard formal semantics for quantification, at least in the sense of offering anything like an explication of our understanding of its meaning.[44] Having so conclusively renounced sets and classes, including the sets and classes familiar from formal semantics, can't we continue to use raw quantification to speak of all propositions, all truths, and the like?

Consider as a first example a proposal offered by Plantinga much in the spirit of the three outlines above.[45] A set of all truths or of all true propositions clearly leads to difficulty. But putting sets aside, can't we speak quantificationally of a *property* shared by all and only those propositions that are in fact true?

It appears not. For consider any property T suggested as filling such a role. Without yet deciding whether T does in fact do what it is supposed to, let us call all those things to which T *does* apply t's. Consider further

1. any property that in fact applies to nothing,

2. all properties that apply to one or more t's, to one or more of the things to which T in fact applies.[46]

We can now show that there are strictly more properties referred to in (1) and (2) than there are t's to which T applies. Suppose any mapping f of t's one-to-one to properties referred to in (1) and (2). Can any such mapping assign a t to every such property? No. For consider the property D:

PROPERTY D   The property of being a t to which $f(t)$—the property it is mapped onto by our chosen f—does not apply.

What t could f map onto property D? None. For suppose D is $f(t^*)$ for some t^*; does $f(t^*)$ apply to t^* or not? If it does, since D applies to only those t for which $f(t)$ does not apply, it does not apply to t^*. If it doesn't, since D applies to all those t for which $f(t)$ does not apply, it *does* apply to t^*. Either alternative, then, gives us a contradiction. There is no way of mapping t's one-to-one to properties referred to in (1) and (2) that doesn't leave some property out; there are *more* such properties than there are t's.

Note, moreover, that for each of the properties referred to in (1) and (2) above, there will be a distinct true proposition, a proposition of the form 'Property p is a property', for instance, or 'Property p is included in (1) or (2)'. There are, then, as many true propositions as there are such properties. But we've also seen that there are more such properties than t's, and thus there must be more true propositions than there are t's—more true propositions than property T, supposed to apply to *all* true propositions, in fact applies to. The basic difficulty facing a set or collection of all truths, it appears, will simply reappear for any *property* proposed in its place.

Can one resist such an argument by denying the diagonal, in this case by denying the existence of the diagonal property D? I think not.[47] On such an approach, we'd be forced to say that the condition laid down at D will simply be an empty condition, a condition without a corresponding property. 'Being a t to which ...' will be a stipulation or specification that fails to define a genuine property.

But here we will still be able to frame an argument to precisely the effect of the original. In the central passage of such an arguent we can show that there are strictly more stipulations or specifications—whether genuinely specifying properties or not—than there are t's. But there will be a distinct true proposition for each of *these*, and thus more true propositions than t's. Whatever property T applies to, we conclude as before, it cannot apply to all true propositions.

Thus the problem seems to grow. If we deny a supposed diagonal property D propertyhood—or, in variations of the argument, deny a proposed diagonal truth D truth or a proposed diagonal proposition D propositionality—we will still want to say what D in each case is instead: a condition that fails to define a genuine property, a mere pseudotruth, an empty logical form that expresses no proposition, or the like. But given *any* answer here, it appears, we will be able to frame a further Cantorian argument of much the same form and to precisely the same effect as the original. There will be more conditions or logical forms or whatever than *t*'s, and thus more truths than any property *T* applies to. These variations seem quite naturally thought of as strengthened forms of the Cantorian argument, analogous to strengthened forms of the Liar.

The important point for my purposes here is simply that such arguments need not rely on any explicit appeal to sets, classes, or other collections. Propositional quantification together with a notion of *properties* seems to give us precisely the same results.

It might be charged, however, that we are still implicitly smuggling set-theoretic notions into such an argument by way of the crucial concepts of mappings or functions, one-to-one correspondences, and cardinality.[48] Even that lingering suggestion of illicit sets can be dispelled, however, by noting that all such notions required in the argument can be defined simply in terms of relations—properties applying to pairs of things—and quantification. A relation *R* gives us a one-to-one mapping from those things that have a property P_1 *into* those things that have a property P_2, for example, just in case

$$\forall x \forall y [P_1 x \ \& \ P_1 y \ \& \ \exists z(P_2 z \ \& \ Rxz \ \& \ Ryz) \to x = y] \ \&$$

$$\forall x [P_1 x \to \exists y \forall z(P_2 z \ \& \ Rxz \equiv z = y)].$$

A relation *R* gives us a mapping from those things that are P_1 that is one-to-one and *onto* those things that are P_2 just in case (here we merely add a conjunct)

$$\forall x \forall y [P_1 x \ \& \ P_1 y \ \& \ \exists z(P_2 z \ \& \ Rxz \ \& \ Ryz) \to x = y] \ \&$$

$$\forall x [P_1 x \to \exists y \forall z(P_2 z \ \& \ Rxz \equiv z = y)] \ \&$$

$$\forall y (P_2 y \to \exists x(P_1 x \ \& \ Rxy)].$$

Relative cardinality can be outlined simply in terms of whether there is a relation that satisfies the first condition and there is not a relation that satisfies the second. Not even here, then, does the basic argument seem to require sets, classes, or other collections; even here propositional quantification with mere properties proves sufficient.

Let us return, however, to another and perhaps more central form of the appeal to raw quantification. To avoid the Cantorian arguments of preceding sections, it appears, we need to renounce not only explicit reference to comprehensive collections of all truths or all propositions but also any reading of a formal semantics for quantification that would implicitly resurrect them. To avoid the Cantorian argument above, it appears, we will also have to abandon any *property* of all truths, and it's clear that a perfectly parallel argument would force us to abandon any property shared by all and only propositions. But suppose we do abandon such global properties, just as we've abandoned corresponding global collections. Will there *then* be any reason to think we can't simply use raw quantification to speak of all propositions?

Unfortunately, the answer is yes. The argument that follows, phrased quantificationally throughout and without either global properties or collections, seems to offer a direct Cantorian argument against universal propositional quantification in general.

In the end, what propositional quantification promises—in the context of possible worlds, a notion of omniscience, or anything else—is a way of speaking about all propositions:

$$\forall p(\ldots p \ldots).$$

But can there be a proposition that is genuinely *about* all propositions?[49]

It appears not. For suppose any such proposition P, and consider all the propositions it is about. These I will term P propositions. Were P genuinely about *all* propositions, of course, there would be a one-to-one mapping f from P propositions to propositions *simpliciter*: a mapping f that assigned P propositions to propositions one-to-one and left no proposition without an assigned P proposition.

But there can be no such mapping. For suppose there were, and consider all P-propositions p such that the proposition to which they are assigned by the chosen mapping f, their $f(p)$, is *not* about them. Certainly we can form a proposition about precisely these—with propositional quantification and 'A' to represent 'about', a proposition of the form

$$\forall p(Pp \mathbin{\&} \sim A(f(p)p) \to \ldots p \ldots).$$

Consider any such proposition P_d. What P proposition could f map onto *it*? None. For consider any P-proposition p^* for which P_d is supposed to be $f(p^*)$. Is P_d about p^* (among other propositions, perhaps) or not?

If P_d *is* about p^*, since P_d is a proposition about precisely those P propositions p such that $f(p)$ is *not* about p, the $f(p^*)$ of p^* cannot be about p^*. The assumption is that P_d *is* about p^*, however, and thus P_d cannot be $f(p^*)$.

If P_d *isn't* about p^*, on the other hand, since P_d is about all P-propositions p such that $f(p)$ is not about p, p^* must be a proposition such that $f(p)$ *is* about p^*. But the assumption is that P_d *isn't* about p^*, and thus P_d cannot be $f(p^*)$.

The chosen function f, then, will map no P proposition onto a proposition P_d. Any one-to-one mapping from P propositions to propositions will thus leave some proposition out: there are *more* propositions than P propositions.

P propositions, however, were taken as simply those propositions an arbitrary proposition P was about. Thus *whatever* propositions any proposition is about, there are more. No proposition can genuinely be about them all.[50]

The truth seems to be that global properties, sets, classes, or other collections are in the end simply inessential to the basic mechanisms of the argument. Appeal to raw quantification proves insufficient to avoid Cantorian conclusions simply because the argument appears with full force phrased quantificationally throughout. That form of the argument offered immediately above, I think, expresses the central difficulties at issue in an illuminatingly condensed form. Here all that seems essential is the use of propositional quantification and the notion that propositions are *about* something. To give that up, it seems, would be to give up the traditional intuitive core of any notion of propositions at all.

Let me finally offer a Cantorian argument against propositional quantification in the still more condensed form of paradox. The paradox—a paradox into which the notion that we *can* speak of *all* propositions seems ineluctably to lead us—consists of two compelling arguments with contradictory conclusions.

Can all propositions be put into one-to-one correspondence with *themselves*?

The answer yes, with its argument, is as follows: Simply assign each proposition to itself. Since

$$\forall p(p = p),$$

we can introduce an identity function f on propositions such that

$$\forall p(f(p) = p).$$

By existential generalization,

$$\exists F \forall p(F(p) = p).$$

And thus, given formal properties of identity,

$\exists F \forall p [\exists r \forall s (F(p) = s \equiv s = r) \, \&$

$\forall q (F(p) = F(q) \rightarrow p = q) \, \&$

$\forall s \exists q (F(q) = s)]$.

What this last symbolic sentence specifies is simply that there is a mapping, one-to-one and onto, from propositions to propositions.[51]

The answer no, with its opposing argument, is as follows:

Consider any F proposed as mapping propositions onto propositions one-to-one, any F such that

$\exists F \forall p [\exists r \forall s (F(p) = s \equiv s = r) \, \&$

$\forall q (F(p) = F(q) \rightarrow p = q) \, \&$

$\forall s \exists q (F(q) = s)]$.

Consider further any propositions p such that the proposition $F(p)$ is not about p, and a proposition about precisely these propositions. This we might envisage as of the form

$\forall p (\sim A(F(p), p) \rightarrow \ldots p \ldots)$.

Take any such proposition P_d. What proposition can F map onto *it*? For what proposition p^* can P_d be $F(p^*)$? None. For consider any p^*. If P_d is about p^*, since P_d is about precisely those propositions p such that $\sim A(F(p), p)$, the $F(p^*)$ of p^* is *not* about p^*. And thus P_d cannot be $F(p^*)$.

If P_d is *not* about p^*, on the other hand, since the only propositions it is not about are those p's such that $A(F(p), p)$, the $F(p^*)$ of p^* *is* about p^*. Since P_d is *not* about p^*, P_d cannot be the $F(p^*)$ of p^*.[52]

In particular, P_d will then be $F(p)$ for no proposition p. Since F was chosen arbitrarily, there can be no mapping of all propositions one-to-one and onto all propositions. More formally,

$\sim \exists F \forall p [\exists r \forall s (F(p) = s \equiv s = r) \, \&$

$\forall q (F(p) = F(q) \rightarrow p = q) \, \&$

$\forall s \exists q (F(q) = s)]$.

What this paradox offers, I think, is a glimpse at the conceptual core of the Cantorian argument we've pursued throughout. All concepts crucial to both sides of the argument appear already in the question it addresses: can all propositions be put into one-to-one correspondence with themselves or not? Once given the resources to ask such a question, it appears, we have all we need to force us to paradox.

It should also be noted that we have here come back to Russell in a sense. If the argument for the negative answer is carried through with identity as a candidate for *F*, the core difficulty becomes whether a proposition about all propositions not about themselves is about itself or not. That, it is fairly clear, is an "aboutness" form of Russell's paradox.

6   A Self-Reflective Problem for the Central Thesis?

I started this chapter with a basic Cantorian argument to the effect that there can be no set of all truths or of all propositions. In the end, however, I offered an argument against universal propositional quantification in general. Isn't there at least a tension between these two conclusions?

In particular, if there can be no genuine propositional quantification, how are we to understand the central claims that there can be no set of all truths or that there can be no set of all propositions? On the face of them, these appear to be claims about all truths or about all propositions, claims to the effect that these fail to form a set. It's at least tempting, then, with '*Sx*' meaning '*x* is a set', to try to represent such claims as follows:

$\sim \exists x(Sx \ \& \ \forall p(Tp \rightarrow p \in x))$

$\sim \exists x(Sx \ \& \ \forall p(p \in x))$

But so represented, of course, such claims would explicitly employ a universal propositional quantification of precisely the form we've seen fall victim to Cantorian argument above.

This tension is merely apparent, I think, though it does have something important to teach us about the central claims at issue throughout. It's merely apparent because my central denials—the denial that there can be any set of all truths, for example, or that there can be any totality of propositions—are emphatically *not* to be understood in the quantificational terms above. What the arguments above ultimately indicate is *not* merely that all truths, somehow unproblematically referred to, fail to form a set. What they show, on the contrary, is that the very notion of *all* truths—or of all propositions or of all that an omniscient being would have to know—is itself incoherent.

For that reason, conclusions throughout should perhaps be rendered using scare quotes or other techniques of indirect speech. There is no "set of all truths," nor for that matter any coherent notion of "all truths," much as there is no such thing as "the square circle" or "the largest positive integer." In each case what we deny is that there is anything that fits a certain description, a description that we would contradict ourselves by straightforwardly *using*. But the denial that there is any such thing as "all truths" or "all propositions" should not itself be thought to commit us to quantifying over all truths or all propositions, any more than the denial that there is such a thing as "the square circle" should be thought to commit us to referring to something as both square and a circle.

In this light it should perhaps be emphasized that the central argument throughout takes the form of a reductio. The logical core is simply that the supposition of an omniscient being, the postulation of a set of all truths, or the assumption of a proposition about all propositions leads directly to contradiction.

That logical core of the argument could perhaps have been presented in a pure form, without any attempt to draw a positive conclusion. In other words, while carefully avoiding even apparent reference to "all truths" or "all propositions," I might have laid out the central abstract patterns of argument at issue as conceptual traps: as mazes bound to lead anyone who *does* take such notions seriously into the tangles of contradiction.

Here I haven't taken that purer course. On the basis of reductio argument I have concluded that the suppositions that lead to contradiction must be denied. I have expressed such denials, and will continue to do so, by saying 'There is no omniscient being', for example, 'There can be no set of all truths', and 'There can be no proposition about all propositions'. Despite some temptations of grammatical form, such denials should ultimately be understood as denials of the coherence of the basic notion of an "omniscient being," or a "set of all truths," or a "proposition about all propositions," rather than as statements somehow intended as about "all truths" or quantifying over "all propositions," for example, and merely to the effect that these fail to form a set.

So understood, I think, the argument against propositional quantification emphatically supports rather than undermines conclusions throughout. What it shows, in fact, is how deep those conclusions really run. The surprise is not merely that "all the truths fail to form a set" or that "all the propositions fail to form a totality." The surprise is that at the point we are tempted to speak of "all truths" or "all propositions," we already face incoherence.

7   Conclusion

Variations on the basic Cantorian argument, we've seen, can be presented against a set of all truths, of all propositions, of those things an omniscient being would have to know, and of the truths appropriate to any possible world. Moreover, the argument effectively holds against intuitive alternatives to sets: against various forms of classes and collections and in systems with or without a power set axiom. The simple Cantorian truth, it appears, is that there can be no complete *totality* of truths. Thought of in terms of its truths, the universe itself must remain open and incomplete.

There is a classic definition of 'set' from Cantor as, "a Many which allows itself to be thought of as a One" (1932, 204). There is also an ancient philosophical problem of the one and the many: do the things of the universe form a one, or a many?

Even in the forms with which I began, the Cantorian argument seems to show that the truths of the universe cannot form a one; there can be no single set, class, collection, or complete totality of all truths. What the arguments of the later sections suggest is that these also cannot be treated as a many. Contradiction seems to follow even if we try to deal with "all truths" or "all propositions" in terms of propositional quantification and entirely in the plural. In that sense, it appears, the universe refuses to be *either* a one or a many.

5 Concluding Notes

1 Philosophical Fragments

In the introduction I began with three philosophical fragments. To summarize and to highlight some remaining questions, I want to return to them here.

As a first fragment I invoked the notion of possible worlds, tracing back to Leibniz and of major importance for the semantics of modal logic and for contemporary metaphysics over the last twenty years. What are possible worlds supposed to be? I have concentrated throughout on one particular approach, according to which possible worlds either are or correspond to maximal consistent sets of propositions. The actual world, on such an account, is or corresponds to a maximal set of all truths.

By the simple Cantorian argument of chapter four, however, reinforced by results in chapters one and three, it appears that there simply *cannot* be any set of all truths. There can be, then, no actual world of the sort that such an account demands, and a variation of the argument will also hold against any such maximal possible world. In the end, moreover, such an argument can be phrased without appeal to sets, classes, or other collections—directly in terms of raw propositional quantification alone. Thus even a purely quantificational variant of such an approach to possible worlds seems to face major Cantorian difficulties.

The second philosophical fragment was this: Gaunilo, in a parody of Anselm's ontological argument for the existence of God, constructed a parallel argument for the existence of the Lost Island, "more excellent than all other lands." Plantinga, in defending a contemporary form of Anselm's argument, attempts to avoid a contemporary form of Gaunilo's. The great-making qualities of islands, Plantinga insists, are without *intrinsic maxima*, and this does not hold for traditional attributes of God:

> The idea of an island than which it's not possible that there be a greater is like the idea of a natural number than which it's not possible that there be a greater.... There neither is nor could be a greatest possible natural number.... And the same goes for islands.... The qualities that make for greatness in islands—numbers of palm trees, amount and quality of coconuts, for example—most of these qualities have no *intrinsic maximum*. That is, there is no degree of productivity or number of palm trees (or of dancing girls) such that it is impossible that an island display more of that quality. So the idea of a greatest possible island is an inconsistent or incoherent idea; it's not possible that there be such a thing....
>
> But doesn't Anselm's argument founder on the same rock? If the idea of a greatest possible island is inconsistent, won't the same hold for the idea of a greatest

possible being? Perhaps not.... Anselm clearly has in mind such properties as wisdom, knowledge, power, and moral excellence or moral perfection. And certainly knowledge, for example, does have an *intrinsic maximum*: if for every proposition *p*, a being *B* knows whether or not *p* is true, then *B* has a degree of knowledge that is utterly unsurpassable. So a greatest possible being would have to have this kind of knowledge: it would have to be *omniscient*. (Plantinga 1974a, 90–91)

What the results of preceding chapters seem to suggest, however, is that knowledge does *not* have any intrinsic maximum of this kind. Here a variety of results converge. As indicated in chapters one and two, forms of both the Liar and Kaplan and Montague's paradox of the Knower suggest that any notion of total knowledge must lead to inconsistency. In chapter three such results were taken further. An omniscient mind would surely be self-reflective in at least the sense of taking its own conceptions of properties as among the things it knows something about. But by an argument patterned on that for expressive incompleteness within formal systems, it appears that no self-reflective mind can be omniscient. There thus can be no omniscient mind. A more fully Gödelian argument can be constructed against omniscience as well. Early in chapter four a simple Cantorian argument was used to show that there can at least be no *set* of all that an omniscient being would have to know. Such a result extends to classes and other collections as well, and in the end, a form of the argument proves applicable against any attempt to outline omniscience in even purely quantificational terms.[1]

As a third fragment I began with the opening lines of the *Tractatus*:

The world is all that is the case.
The world is the totality of facts, not of things.
The world is determined by the facts, and by their being *all* the facts.

Perhaps the central theme that runs throughout the results we've considered is that there ultimately can be no totality of facts. If so, of course, there can be no closed world of the form the *Tractatus* demands.

The line of argument has been complicated enough that one must be wary of dogmatic and precipitate conclusions. One may legitimately wonder whether some new response, or some variation on an old one, might yet offer a way out. Nonetheless the investigation has also been a wide and comprehensive one, and its basic lesson may be precisely what it seems: that within any logic we have, there simply can be no coherent notion of total knowledge or total truth.

2   Within Any Logic We Have ...

My arguments throughout have clearly employed, and in that sense clearly rely on, contemporary logic as we know it. Surely there is no alternative: we would be satisfied with nothing less than what contemporary logic has to offer, and we cannot reach magically beyond our history for something more. As noted in the introduction, however, this reliance on contemporary logic should perhaps be made explicit in the conclusions throughout: *within any logic we have*, it appears, there can be no coherent notion of total knowledge or of a totality of truths.

The loophole this seems to leave open is, of course, the following: Perhaps contemporary logic is merely inadequate to do justice to a notion of total knowledge or truth. Perhaps some other logic, dramatically different in form, *would* admit a coherent notion of omniscience and *would* allow a totality of truth.

What gives this response some power is the fact that the results considered throughout flirt quite openly with paradox, and paradox has bred new logics before. Perhaps it could be done again. Perhaps, despite appearances, it would be possible, for example, technically to specify a "gob" or a "bunch" that would both coherently and intuitively collect or cover "all truths" in a way that neither sets nor classes nor even raw quantification evidently can. Perhaps.

In a final section I want to offer some speculations as to what the actual development of such a new logic might *mean*. As things stand, however, it must be recognized that we neither have any such logic nor have any good guesses as to what any such logic could look like. The 'perhaps' above is at best a mere promissory note, a second or third mortgage on a merely hoped-for totality of truths.

There are a number of reasons, moreover, to think that the loophole of a new logic is smaller than it might at first appear. One is simply that alternative logical options *have* been considered at every relevant point throughout the study: proposals for multivalued, infinitely valued, gapped, glutted, and deviant logics; amplified, amputated, and alternative set and class theories; hierarchical, nonfoundational, fixed-point, schematic-indexical, and redundancy theories of truth. In all such cases our results have been uniformly negative. Thus as a real possibility, as opposed to the easy promise of an empty possibility, actual construction of some new logic with any chance at all of resolving the difficulties at issue could hardly be more daunting.

It should also be emphasized how forceful our conclusions really are. Consider again, for example, the simple result that there can be no set of all truths. Here the result is not merely that a set of all truths isn't included in set theory or its simple extensions, as if it might conveniently be added as an afterthought. It is not simply that a set of all truths can't be characterized within the language of such systems, as if it might nonetheless linger tantalizingly just beyond the edge of effability.[2] It is rather that, given the fundamental principles of set theory and the simplest of intuitions regarding truth, there is not and cannot be any set of all truths.

In the end, of course, these results go well beyond the case of sets. What they show is not that our logic leaves out a totality of truths or a notion of "all truths" but that, given fundamental logical principles, there cannot *be* any such totality, there can be no consistent notion of "all truths." Given fundamental logical principles, the notion of total knowledge must prove similarly impossible; it is not simply omitted, not transcendentally ineffable, but logically incoherent.

The apparent loophole was the following: Perhaps contemporary logic is merely inadequate to do justice to a notion of total knowledge or a totality of truths. Perhaps some other logic would be adequate. But note finally that this same response could be made in behalf of *any* position, however ludicrous, and in the face of *any* argument, however rigorous. Perhaps our logic is merely inadequate to do justice to real circular squares or married bachelors. As things stand, then, such a response does nothing to distinguish a notion of total knowledge or total truth from any of the various incoherent notions that may fall victim to logical argument.

3   Some Twilight Speculations

Appeal to a mere possibility of some new logic, we have seen, will hardly do as a *reply* to the arguments throughout. Here I want nonetheless to take at least the *idea* of such a logic quite seriously.

Suppose for a moment that we *were* to see some elegant and powerful new logic, a logic as yet undreamt of, built to address the problems I have raised, in ways we can't as yet imagine. How might the existence of such a logic change these results, or our reading of these results, throughout? What would the creation of such a logic *mean*?

Here I have only speculations, and no arguments, to offer. That said, however, I think the following is a quite plausible prospect.

Were we actually to develop such a logic, we might well face a bifurcation within philosophical and logical theory. We would perhaps be forced to choose either to retain logic as we know it and the incomplete universe it seems to entail or to opt for a new logic that might promise a universe finished and complete but that would also predictably sacrifice some major portion of traditional logic and would thus offer a universe logically disorienting and unfamiliar in other regards.

Such a bifurcation, were it to develop, might parallel divergences between standard and nonstandard arithmetics or between Euclidean and non-Euclidean geometries. Here, as there, I think, the alternatives could be expected to be coldly exclusive. Here, as there, our options would be dramatically different—a choice between logical spaces as different as the physical spaces of Euclid and Riemann.

A logico-philosophical bifurcation of this kind might carry further implications as well. Standard and nonstandard arithmetics ultimately offer divergent views of what numbers *are*, and our conception of what *arithmetic* is has inevitably changed as a consequence. The mere existence of alternative geometries has made the enterprise of geometry itself a different discipline—a matter no longer of intuiting a priori essential properties of space but of tracking the implications of speculative spatial hypotheses.

A logico-philosophical bifurcation of the sort envisaged, I think, might have similar important lessons to offer regarding philosophical reflection and the discipline of formal logic. These might come to be seen as something less than investigations of an independent and binding logical reality. At the same time, however, they might come to be valued as something more: creative modes of conceptual freedom.

Notes

Introduction

1. See, for example, Adams 1974, 211–231, and Alvin Plantinga's treatment of worlds in terms of books in Plantinga 1974b, 44–69, and 1974a, 35–44.
2. For further work on Plantinga and Gaunilo, see Grim 1979 and 1982.

Chapter 1

1. Its most significant rival in antiquity is perhaps the sorites, or paradox of the heap, credited along with the Liar to Eubulides. See William Kneale and Mary Kneale 1962, 114 ff.
2. David Grossman has pointed out that a similar problem will arise in terms of (i) for any supposed set Φ of all falsehoods:

(i) is a member of Φ.   (i)

3. By essentially the same reasoning, it can be argued that there is nothing to which all and only truths stand in any particular relation. For consider any U (for 'universe') and relation R such that all and only truths are supposed to stand in relation R to U. Does (ii) stand in relation R to U, or not?

(ii) does not stand in relation R to U.   (ii)

4. In these arguments parenthesized numbers, '(4)' and '(5)', are to be understood as applying to at least potential *truths*. In arguments below they are used to refer to candidates for propositions and possible objects of truth. I leave to section 6, however, a more complete discussion of sentences and propositions.
5. See also Alvin Plantinga's treatment of worlds in terms of books in 1974a, 35–44, and 1974b, 44–69, and John Pollock's discussion of such an approach in 1984, 43–98. Something very like Adams' and Plantinga's "maximality" approach to possible worlds appears to trace all the way back to Leibniz (see in particular Brown 1987).

This is not, of course, the only way that possible worlds have been introduced. In Lewis 1973, for example, possible worlds are ways things might have been. In Stalnaker 1976 they are also "ways things might have been," but Stalnaker envisages the "ways" as abstract entities in their own right. In Slote 1975 they are possible histories of the world. Though none of these alternatives is outlined in terms of a maximality condition as explicit as that in Plantinga and in Adams, it might be argued that such a condition is implicitly required in these accounts as well.

Adams' propositions are lettered here rather than numbered so as to avoid conflict with the text.
6. This phrasing is perhaps closest to Plantinga's.
7. All that is of importance throughout the present work is that an omniscient being believe all and only truths. Even this minimal condition, however, has not always been met in philosophical attempts to define omniscience. The following, for example, is quite clearly the standard definition in the literature:

DEFINITION 1   A being x is *omniscient* $=_{df}$ for all p, p is true iff x knows that p.

This is for example Peter Geach's definition (1977), and it is equivalent in all essentials to definitions offered by A. N. Prior (1962), Richard Swinburne (1977), William E. Mann (1975), Plantinga (1974a), and Tomberlin and McGuinness (1977).

Despite such unanimity, however, omniscience so defined will clearly not do, at least without supplement, as an adequate characterization of the knowledge of a traditional God.

What seems quite generally to have gone unrecognized is that a being might qualify as omniscient in this sense and yet hold any number of *false* beliefs.

Consider a being B with false beliefs $p_1, p_2, \ldots, p_n$. Since B cannot be said to *know* any of these, the definition above does not require that *these* beliefs be *true*. So long as B also believes and knows all *truths*, he will qualify as omniscient, despite his false beliefs. What definition 1 requires, after all, is simply that all truths be known by an omniscient being and that all things known by such a being be true. Since falsehoods believed by such a being are neither truths nor things known by such a being, the standard definition effectively puts no restrictions on the false beliefs of an omniscient being.

To qualify as omniscient and yet hold false beliefs, B would, of course, have to hold contradictory beliefs as well. Given any false p_k that B believes, B would also have to believe that it was not the case that p_k, since B knows, and so of course believes, all truths. Since an omniscient being is required to know *all* truths, moreover, such a being would have to know that his beliefs *were* contradictory in such a case. But none of this shows that a being so flawed as to hold contradictory beliefs, or so flawed as to shamelessly recognize that he holds contradictory beliefs, might not nonetheless qualify as omniscient in the sense of definition 1. Nothing in that definition requires that an omniscient being avoid even blatant contradiction.

If we are to say that a traditional God is omniscient in the sense of definition 1, then, we will at least have to say something more as well. We will have to add that God holds no false beliefs, perhaps, or insist that he is not only omniscient but also "omnirational" in some sense that excludes the possibility of contradictory beliefs.

Such difficulties can be more straightforwardly avoided, I think, by using a definition such as the following:

DEFINITION 2   A being x is *omniscient* $=_{df}$ for all p, p is true iff x believes that p AND x believes that p iff x knows that p.

Here AND is capitalized to indicate it is the main connective between two biconditionals. Unlike definition 1, definition 2 does satisfy the minimal condition that an omniscient being believes all and only truths, and moreover, it ensures that such a being knows all that he believes. (Here, see also Grim 1983 and critical discussion in Kvanvig 1986.)

Definition 2 still demands universal quantification over all propositions, of course. Some quite general difficulties for propositional quantification are raised in chapter four.

8. In personal correspondence Roy A. Sorensen has phrased the argument as follows. Consider (A):

I do not believe (A).   (A)

Sentence (A) is paradoxical insofar as it appears to force me into endless vacillation. If I believe (A), then I should not believe (A) because my belief in (A) ensures its falsity. On the other hand, if I do not believe (A), I should believe it because my lack of belief ensures its truth. (A) is anti-incorrigible; I must be mistaken about it (whether commissively or omissively).

The anti-incorrigibility of (A) is surprising. But surprises in themselves are not philosophically interesting. What is philosophically interesting is the exposure of inconsistent beliefs which are responsible for the surprise. Given that (A) is semantically satisfactory, suspicion falls on some of our epistemic principles. There are three candidates. First, there is a principle of self-awareness: one is aware of one's doxastic states. In other words, if one believes p, then one believes that one believes that p, and if one neither believes nor disbelieves p, then one believes that one neither believes nor disbelieves p. Second, there is the principle of deductive closure; if one believes that p, then one believes all of the consequences of p. Third, there is the principle of direct consistency; one cannot both believe a proposition and believe its negation. Few philosophers believe that these principles apply to ordinary people. The principles are only intended to apply to ideal thinkers. The idealization is motivated by the fact that our normative standards for appraising beliefs appear to embody these principles. In any case, let us now turn to the question of how an ideal thinker would respond to a sentence such as (A). Unlike me, the ideal thinker does not tire out or make logical errors. His freedom from epistemic flaw generates a contradiction. Either he believes (A) or he does not. If he believes (A), then his self-awareness guarantees that he also believes that he believes (A). The ideal thinker's deductive closure then guarantees that he infers from his belief in (A), the falsehood of (A). So the ideal thinker will both believe and disbelieve (A). But this violates the ideal thinker's requirement of consistency. Now suppose that the ideal thinker does not believe (A). Self-awareness ensures that he will believe that he does not believe (A). Deductive closure ensures that he will then infer from this lack of belief in (A), the truth of (A). The ideal thinker will then both believe and not believe (A). So once again, a contradiction arises. We should therefore conclude that such an ideal thinker is impossible.

With regard to relatives of the Divine Liar, see also Routley 1981.

9. C. S. Peirce maintained that "reality depends on the ultimate decision of the community" and that "the opinion which is fated to be ultimately agreed to by all who investigate, is what we mean by the truth." See especially Peirce 1868, Peirce 1878, and Rescher 1978, 19–39. A similar view appears in some of Hilary Putnam's work. See especially Putnam 1978 and Millikan 1986.

10. "Personal paradoxes" akin to (9) were pointed out to me years ago by David Boyer. They also put in a brief appearance in Whitely 1962, 61–62, and figure prominently in Sorensen 1984 and 1988.

11. Such approaches appear in a number of forms in Robert L. Martin's two excellent collections (Martin 1978a and 1984).

Because gapped and many-valued approaches face essentially the same difficulty, the Strengthened Liar, I treat them together here. Indeed, one in general can formally treat gapped approaches as variations on a many-valued strategy, using, for example, many-valued matrices such as those below (though it must then be admitted that 'many-*valued*' is a misnomer). On vexed and vexing questions of formal and philosophical distinctions between gapped and many-valued approaches, see Haack 1974a, 55–64.

12. With regard to set-theoretic examples such as

(i) is not a member of set Θ,   (i)

it should perhaps be noted that gapped and three-valued responses to set-theoretic paradoxes standardly fall afoul of strengthened forms. Here, see Rescher 1969, 206–212, and Maypole 1975.

13. The use of such an operator is of significant technical interest in its own right. By a result of V. I. Shestakov, any finitely many-valued logic can be dealt with in terms of an operator Vvp subject to axiomatic stipulations and the standard two-valued connectives (see Zinov'ev 1963, 38–40, and Rescher 1969, 77–80). This alone does not argue for any supremacy of the standard two-valued system, however, since it is also the case that the standard two-valued system can be constructed within various systems of many-valued logic.

14. Here for simplicity I've used '$/VTF/$', for example, to indicate the value of a statement attributing truth to a statement that is in fact false. Technically, of course, the 'F' position should be filled with some device indicating a proposition with a value F rather than the value itself.

15. As Rescher notes (1969, 88), some three-valued "solutions" to the Liar succeed in assigning (13) a value but face paradox again in (14). The matrix used here escapes this difficulty as well.

16. Rescher 1969, 89.

Here a historical note is perhaps in order. In 1939 D. A. Bochvar introduced a three-valued logic designed explicitly to escape the Liar. Within that system, in its "internal" form, the relevant form of the Liar could not consistently be assumed to be either T or F but could consistently be assumed to be I. In Bochvar's system, however, I was infectious—any compound sentence having some component with the value I took on the value I as well. Thus no compound sentences came out T for all value assignments to their components; Bochvar's internal system allowed for no tautologies whatsoever.

In an attempt to regain tautologies, Bochvar supplemented the internal system with an auxiliary "external assertion operator" and corresponding "external" connectives. With that addition, all classical tautologies reappear on the external level. But paradox does as well—Bochvar's system falls victim to a form of the Strengthened Liar.

17. Another way of putting the point is this. We could technically avoid the Strengthened Liar by means of a three-valued matrix that violates the conditions outlined above—one with additional T's in the left column, for example, or values other than T along the diagonal. But this says nothing in favor of three- or many-valued logics, for we might also have "avoided" the standard Liar by violating precisely these conditions in a two-valued matrix. Consider, for example, the following matrices:

Two-value matrix for Vvp

	p	
v	T	F
T	T	F
F	F	F

Two-value matrix for Vvp

	p	
v	T	F
T	T	F
F	T	T

The matrix on the left violates the diagonal condition. That on the right violates the left-column condition. But given either matrix, the standard Liar can be assigned a univocal value: F by the left matrix, T by the right. This is clearly unsatisfactory as a solution to the Liar, however. For the same reasons, violation of the same conditions are unsatisfactory as a three-valued solution to the Strengthened Liar.

18. Similar conclusions will, of course, hold for the other forms of the Bionic Liar above. For example, (20) gives us

$/(20)/ = /(20) \neq 1/.$

If we assign (20) a value of 1, $/1 \neq 1/$ will then take a value of 1. If we assign (20) a value v_n other than 1, $/(20)/$ will equal $/v_n \neq 1/$. To make this viable, it appears, we would be forced to the unpalatable expedient of interpreting '$=$' so that only for some v_n other than 1 does $/v_n = 1/$ equal 1.

19. Whether it is the sentences themselves that are taken to express propositions in a given context or particular utterances or inscriptions of such sentences will not be of major importance.

20. See, for example, Garver 1978. Further literature on the position appears in Haack 1978, 140.

In a variation on the position that doesn't explicitly use the term 'propositions', one might claim that sentences in particular occurrences are the proper bearers of truth, rather than sentences themselves, and that some sentences in some occurrences say nothing. Here I am obliged to David Boyer and participants in a departmental colloquium at St. Cloud University.

21. Brian Skyrms takes such a position in 1978a, ultimately concluding that the principle of substitutivity of identity must be rejected.

22. Indeed, such theories are quite generally forced to incorporate restrictions for the explicit purpose of blocking paradoxes—paradoxes, for example, regarding a property of non-self-applicability. Those restrictions are in turn borrowed from other approaches to the Liar that are not essentially "propositional" in the sense at issue here. Zalta (1983), for example, relies on a new kind of type theory, while Turner (1987) borrows a theory of Gupta and Herzberger in roughly the hierarchical tradition. Bealer (1982) defers the problem by restricting himself to a first-order theory as long as possible, ultimately suggesting an iterative and context-relative approach in the manner of Burge. On property theories in general, see also Cocchiarella 1989 and Bealer and Mönnich 1989.

23. This objection is well put in Haack 1978, 140.

24. See Post 1973, 1974, 1979 and Anderson 1978.

25. This difficulty for propositional approaches to the Liar is well put in Martin 1978b.

26. Johnstone seems to hold such a position in 1981.

For simplicity I will occasionally speak in what follows of a sentence as simply true rather than as "expressing a true proposition."

27. Here my guess is that a propositionalist would be forced to say that '(25)' in (26) *has* a referent, whereas '(25)' in (25) does not. I am grateful to David Boyer and participants in a departmental colloquium at St. Cloud University for bringing this point to my attention.

28. The notion of a set of rules for picking proposition-expressing from propositionless sentences was introduced on p. 21. One lesson of the result here seems to be that hope for such a set of rules—at least for any set of rules effectively applicable to sentences on sight and on the basis of obvious structural features—must prove a vain and empty hope. For were there such a set of rules, it would give us a technique for magically divining all truths.

29. Priest 1979, 220. See also Priest 1987.

30. See especially da Costa 1974; Routley 1982; Routley, Meyer, Plumwood, and Brady 1982; and Priest, Routley, and Norman 1989.

To escape paradox in general on such an approach, however, a great deal of logic—not only of classical logic but also of intuitionistic and even relevance logic—would have to be sacrificed. Here Curry's paradox is particularly demanding. See Meyer, Routley, and Dunn 1979 and Myhill 1975.

31. "*There simply is no need* for us to lapse into inconsistency ourselves in order to realize those objectives for which inconsistency-tolerant logics have traditionally been devised" (Rescher and Brandom 1979, 139).

32. Rescher and Brandom 1979, 35. On Rescher and Brandom, see also Dale 1984.

33. See Priest 1984, 160. Here I simply follow Priest in speaking of sentences themselves as true or false.

34. See Priest 1979, 238–239.

35. Here I simplify significantly; in Russell 1903 not all variables are restricted to single types, for example. For a more complete treatment, see Copi 1971.

36. Here again I simplify. For a more textually scrupulous treatment, see especially Chihara 1972 and Copi 1971 and 1979.

37. See Copi 1979, 349.

38. Russell quite explicitly draws the conclusion that "'all propositions' and 'all properties' are meaningless phrases" (1908, 155).

39. Here, see also Chihara 1973.

40. Tarski 1935. On the relation between Russell's and Tarski's treatments, see also Church 1976.

41. A similar hierarchy of knowledge predicates is suggested in Anderson 1983.

42. See Copi 1979, 353.

43. Each of these charges is made effectively in Kripke 1975. See also Haack 1978, 143–145.

44. This is the definition sketched in note 7. Here any of various definitions might be used, however. For present purposes, all that is important is that a definition of omniscience in one way or another takes the form $\forall p(\ldots p$ is true$\ldots)$. Some quite general difficulties regarding propositional quantification are raised in chapter four.

45. It should perhaps be noted, however, that Kripke does not commit himself to any particular three-valued approach; he merely notes weak and strong Kleene systems and van Fraassen's supervaluations as possible options.

46. Here a partial logic such as weak or strong Kleene or van Fraassen supervaluations is assumed in order to deal, for example, with disjunctions with only one disjunct that has been assigned a truth value.

47. Hans Herzberger and Anil Gupta have explored similar but nonmonotonic progressions. See Herzberger 1982, Gupta 1982, and Visser 1989.

48. Kripke 1975, 701–705; a result anticipated in Martin and Woodruff 1975.

49. This difficulty remains whether we conceive of our metalanguage as bivalent, as Kripke suggests (1975, 714) or as "gapped" in the sense of the original hierarchy. In a bivalent metalanguage (51) will function as a form of the Liar. In a gapped metalanguage it will function as a form of the Strengthened Liar.

50. As indicated in note 47, Herzberger 1982 and Gupta 1982 offer what might be considered nonmonotonic hierarchies. Gupta, for example—important details aside—offers a (bivalent) hierarchy in terms of progressive applications of a rule of revision. Truth values for Liar-like sentences remain unstable throughout. In such an approach, however, 'is not stably true' is in much the position of Kripke's 'is false or ungrounded' and appears to demand a similar treatment in terms of ascending metalanguages or something equally incomplete. It thus appears that such an account can offer no more hope than does Kripke's for a notion of *all* truth or omniscience.

51. Despite inclusion of non-well-founded sets, ZFC/AFA doesn't offer any particularly new treatment for either Cantor's set of all sets $\{x \mid x = x\}$ or Russell's set of all non-self-membered sets $\{x \mid x \notin x\}$. Within the basic conception of ZFC/AFA, as in other theories, these can appear at best only as proper classes.

52. Formulas of any of the following forms I take as atomic:

(**a Has c**), where **a** is the name **Max** or **Claire** and **c** is a card name;

(**a Believes th**), where **th** is a propositional demonstrative;

True(th).

L-formulas as a whole consist of the smallest collection containing atomic formulas and closed under the following formation rules:

If ϕ and ψ are formulas, so are (**ϕ & ψ**), (**ϕ $\vee$ ψ**), and ~ϕ.

If ϕ is a formula, so is (**True ϕ**) and (**a Believes ϕ**), where **a** is **Claire** or **Max**.

53. More formally, we take the closure Γ of a set of atomic propositions *AtPROP* under (infinite) conjunction and disjunction as the basic set *PROP* of propositions. *AtPROP* is the largest class such that if $p \in AtPROP$, p is of one of the forms

$[a\,H\,c]$ or $\overline{[a\,H\,c]}$, where a is Claire or Max and c is a card;

$[a\,Bel\,g]$ or $\overline{[a\,Bel\,g]}$, where $g \in \Gamma(AtPROP)$;

$[Tr\,g]$ or $\overline{[Tr\,g]}$, where $g \in \Gamma(AtPROP)$.

Taking the largest such class guarantees that we include all relevant "circular" propositions provided for within ZFC/AFA.

54. Barwise and Etchemendy note, in fact, that their Russellian account is ultimately quite close to Kripke's: "Our notion of an almost semantically closed model is just a fixed point requirement on truth, of the kind Kripke endorses, and our proof of the Closure Theorem corresponds closely to his construction of a least fixed point (1987, 86). Their account does differ from Kripke's in the circular phenomena allowed by the use of Aczel set theory. As elegant and important as that addition is, however, it does not change in any essential way the lessons drawn regarding hierarchical approaches above. In particular, both in Barwise and Etchemendy's Russellian account and in Kripke's, the fact that the Liar is *not* true seems to be a fact that fails to be included in any totality.

55. 'Largest classes' here guarantees that all desired circular objects from ZFC/AFA will be included.

56. Note that to say that a situation is not of type $[H, \text{Claire}, 3\clubsuit, 1]$ is not to say it is of the dual type $[H, \text{Claire}, 3\clubsuit, 0]$.

57. At the point at which Barwise and Etchemendy broach this difficulty, they in fact offer two options: that sketched above, which seems to do at least rough justice to pretheoretic intuitions regarding situations, and an alternative in which the difficulty is written off as a mere side effect of their formal modeling. On this alternative, "Where the world comes in … is in determining what the facts are in a given real situation, and so what its appropriate set-theoretic counterpart is. In other words, if the world were different, the same situation would be modeled by a different set-theoretic object, a different member of *SIT*" (1987, 129). But on this second notion of situation it's far from clear how situations are to be identified across possibilities. Barwise and Etchemendy note that this "is analogous to what happens when we model properties with sets: the same set could not have had different members, though the same property could well have applied to different things" (1987, 129). But the fact that similar problems appear in modeling properties with sets is hardly satisfying. Because of such modal difficulties, we've learned that properties *can't* plausibly be thought of as sets. A similarly fundamental problem seems to arise here in thinking of situations set-theoretically.

58. On sets, classes, and Cantorian difficulties for Barwise and Etchemendy's notion of the world as a "collection of all facts," see Grim and Mar 1989.

59. Within the Austinian account there cannot, in fact, even be *states of affairs* regarding the world. The immediate reason is that soa's are specifically outlined only for Claire, Max, the cards, and a range of propositions. But there is also a deeper reason: states of affairs are to be modeled as sets, but the world as a whole is a proper or ultimate class. As such it cannot appear as a member of any set and thus cannot be included in any state of affairs.

60. In a postscript to *The Liar*, Barwise and Etchemendy also outline very briefly a third account, designed to use a reflection theorem and inherent limitations of the Russellian account to save the Austinian approach from at least some of the objections raised above. Here I won't introduce the technicalities of the reflection theorem itself; all that is crucial is that as far as expressible propositions go, any Russellian model M can be mirrored by an Austinian situation m.

> It seems clear that we sometimes use sentences to describe limited parts of the world; indeed, most of our everyday claims are of just this sort. On the other hand, it also seems possible to express claims about the world as a whole….

We could amend our Austinian model to reflect this point of view in various ways. One way would be to use the mirrors produced by the Reflection Theorem to get around the set/class problem. Let *m* be any mirror. By an *m-proposition* we will mean a proposition whose truth or falsity is a fact in *m*. By an *m-situation* we mean a situation which is both a constituent of a proposition in *m* and also a subset of *m*. An alternative model of the Austinian perspective would take *m* to represent the whole world, and so would allow only *m*-propositions and *m*-situations. With this technique, we would find that certain sentences would express propositions about the world as a whole, while others would not. Among the latter is the Liar sentence, of course.... We have shown that if it is used to make a claim about some particular portion of the world, it always gives you a fact that lies outside the portion being described. Consequently, it simply cannot be used to make a claim about the world as a whole, whether or not other sentences can be so used." (1987, 188–189)

Every Russellian model *M* is incomplete in the sense that although it *makes* its Liar proposition false, the falsity of the Liar is not itself included in *M*. In the approach sketched above, the 'whole world' is relegated to an Austinian mirror of such a model, and thus it would seem that any inherent incompleteness of Russellian models would simply be reflected in their Austinian mirrors.

The only sense in which this is *not* the case relies on the fact that the class of "propositions," for example, has here been cut back to include only those propositions true or false *in M*. "Situations" have also been cut back accordingly. Technically, then, we can no longer speak of a situation or fact of the Liar's falsity being omitted from *m*. Though the Liar is still false, there is no longer any proposition that might express its falsehood, nor any situation of its being false that is even a candidate for inclusion in *m*.

It is dubious that this could serve as a satisfactory response to the uneasiness regarding an incomplete Russellian world that initially motivated Barwise and Etchemendy's attempt at an Austinian alternative. With regard to the Russellian approach, they remark, "Once we see that the Liar really *isn't* true, it seems that this fact should itself be a genuine feature of the world, a feature capable of influencing the truth or falsity of propositions. But of course it cannot be" (1987, 105). Any intuitive dissatisfaction with the incompleteness of a Russellian approach will hardly be assuaged by one's being told that the perceived falsity of the Liar is no longer even regarded as a *potential* fact or situation for inclusion in the world. Whatever it is, it will be left out. What we've done is simply to erect a Russellian model within the Austinian, dub it 'the world', and refuse by terminological sleight to recognize whatever lies outside it as worthy of propositional or factual status.

It's also clear that major advantages claimed for the Austinian approach over the Russellian disappear on this revision. In touting the virtues of the Austinian account, Barwise and Etchemendy write,

> Taken together, the above considerations suggest that we think of the Austinian conception of language and its relation to the world as a kind of completion of the simpler, Russellian conception. That is, we can think of the Russellian's world as simply *part* of the real total world, a part that a proposition can be about. Of course it cannot encompass everything there is, and so there remain facts that the Austinian can both grasp and express, but which lie beyond the scope of the Russellian. Thus what initially appears to be an expressive limitation of Austinian propositions is actually a reflection of their greater expressive power, their ability to reach beyond the fixed boundaries imposed by the Russellian conception. (1987, 155–156)

On this third account, any such virtue will, of course, be lost.

The one apparent gain of the third approach is that the "world" *will* be something that at least some proposition can be about, since that term is now applied to a mere situation. Nonetheless, paradox will remain. Within an expanded language in the spirit of the third account, the following sentence, for example, will continue to pose all the same essential difficulties:

'Appended to its own quotation cannot be used to express a true proposition about the world as a whole' appended to its own quotation cannot be used to express a true proposition about the world as a whole.

Chapter 2

1. Kaplan and Montague 1960. See also Anderson 1983 and Burge 1984.

2. Montague 1963. A form of Montague's argument against syntactical treatments of indirect discourse appears in Thomason 1977, and another form against certain psychologically motivated semantic theories appears in Thomason 1980. Some of these applications of the Knower have been contested with a hierarchical treatment in mind in Skyrms 1978b and Burge 1984. An interesting recent attempt, using predicates that mirror the limitations of operators, appears in Rivières and Levesque 1986.

3. Implications for necessity, though perhaps tempting throughout, I leave for consideration elsewhere.

4. See, for example, Boolos and Jeffrey 1989, 158.

5. Somewhat more strictly, if we use $\bar{A}$ for the Gödel numeral corresponding to the Gödel number $\#A$ for formula A, '$\triangle(\bar{A})$' can be read as 'The formula with Gödel number $\#A$ is known to be true.'

6. For the moment I will act as if such claims in their full generality were added to the list. In fact, however, only particular instances of these are required for the argument below.

7. The proof, omitted from the text for purposes of simplicity, is essentially as follows.
   For any expression A, let the *diagonalization* of A be the further expression $\exists x(x = \bar{A}\ \&\ A)$, and let *diag* be the function that, for any Gödel number n of an expression, gives $diag(n)$ as the Gödel number of the diagonalization of that expression.
   To make a long story short, *diag* will be a recursive function, and all recursive functions are *represented* in Q and hence in Q'. The function *diag* will thus be represented in Q': there will be an expression $A(x, y)$ of Q' such that for any n, k, if $diag(n) = k$, $\vdash_{Q'} \forall y(A(\boldsymbol{n}, y) \equiv y = \boldsymbol{k})$, where $\boldsymbol{n}$ and $\boldsymbol{k}$ are numerals for numbers n and k respectively.
   Let F be the expression $\exists y(A(x, y)\ \&\ B(y))$, and let n be the Gödel number of F. Let G be the further expression $\exists x(x = \boldsymbol{n}\ \&\ \exists y(A(x, y)\ \&\ B(y)))$. Since $\boldsymbol{n} = \bar{F}$, G is the diagonalization of F. G will also be logically equivalent to $\exists y(A(\boldsymbol{n}, y)\ \&\ B(y))$, and thus $\vdash_{Q'} G \equiv \exists y(A(\boldsymbol{n}, y)\ \&\ B(y))$. Now let k be the Gödel number of expression G. Then $diag(n) = k$ and $\boldsymbol{k} = \bar{G}$.

So $\vdash_{Q'} \forall y(A(\boldsymbol{n}, y) \equiv y = \boldsymbol{k})$.
So $\vdash_{Q'} G \equiv \exists y(y = \boldsymbol{k}\ \&\ B(y))$.
So $\vdash_{Q'} G \equiv B(\boldsymbol{k})$,   i.e., $\vdash_{Q'} G \equiv B(\bar{G})$.

This form of the proof is taken from Boolos and Jeffrey 1980, 172–173. A generalized form of the diagonal lemma appears in Boolos 1979, 49.

8. Another way of getting the same result result is to prove initially a variation on the diagonal lemma, which gives us $\vdash_{Q'} G \equiv B(\sim G)$. In one form, such a proof simply adds a few well-placed negations to the reasoning of note 7 above.
   On the interpretation sketched so far, of course, '$S \equiv \triangle(\overline{\sim S})$' says in effect 'my negation is known' in the same (rough) sense that the standard Gödel sentence says 'I am not a theorem'.

9. My comments here are directed at "something like" Hintikka's system rather than at Hintikka's work per se. For one thing, Hintikka's 'K' appears as an operator rather than as a predicate of sentences. Recourse to operators is further discussed in sections 4 and 5.

10. This is Hintikka's original gloss of 'Kap' in 1967, 29. Later in the same work he proposes a reinterpretation: that 'Kap' should perhaps be read not as 'a knows that p' but 'It follows from what a knows that p.'

11. Various modifications have been proposed. See, for example, Eberle 1974, Moore and Hendrix 1979, Konolige 1984, Cresswell 1973, Rantala 1982, Rescher and Brandom 1979, chap. 19, Levesque 1984, and Fagin and Halpern 1985.

12. Hintikka 1967, 36. He has since changed his tune. Hintikka now emphasizes that difficulty for the principle at issue arises only if we take every epistemically possible world to be logically possible. See Taylor 1983 and Hintikka 1975.

13. One obvious candidate for a predicate with these schemata is 'is necessary'. In 1977 Richmond Thomason lists other plausible candidates: 'is certain', 'can be demonstrated', 'follows from what I know', 'logic alone suffices to establish', and 'is trivial'. Certain deontic notions also seem plausible candidates here, though I leave exploration of deontic forms of the Knower to others or to another context.

14. Here a contrast with Tarski's theorem is perhaps also in order. What Tarski shows in 1935 is in effect that the schema

$$\triangle(\bar{A}) \equiv A$$

cannot consistently be added to the axioms of Q'. As Montague notes in 1963, however, the schemata of the Knower seem intuitively much weaker than this, and in that regard the argument of the Knower is the more powerful result.

15. Alternatively, if something is a member of α, it actually obtains.

16. Here I have not reserved a separate section for possible three-valued and "gapped" responses. In addition to fairly extensive treatment of them in chapter one, see note 20 below.

17. Anderson 1983. Despite its name, however, Anderson's Strengthened Knower is most closely related not to the Strengthened Liar but to the Propositional Liar, outlined in chapter one.

18. An expression relation of very much this type is introduced in Parsons 1974.

19. We might go on to treat propositions as sets of possible worlds, for example, or as equivalence classes of sentences under a synonymy relation (see Anderson 1983, 346–347). The point is simply that the symbolic treatment here demands no particular interpretation for propositions.

20. Here, as before, only particular instances of these schemata are in fact required for the argument.

21. Here I haven't reserved a section for three-valued and "gapped" responses to the Knower. These too fall afoul of a form of the Strengthened Knower, however, much as three-valued and gapped responses to the Liar were seen to fall afoul of the Strengthened Liar in chapter one.

Suppose that a proponent of a three-valued or gapped response claims that knowledge or truth properly applies only to sentences with (classical) truth values and that some of the sentences to which '$\triangle$' is applied in the argument fail to qualify. The self-referential '$\sim S$' in '$S \equiv \triangle(\sim S)$', for example, should perhaps be rejected either as having some third value or as lacking a truth value entirely.

To incorporate this proposal into the language, let us use p as a variable reserved exclusively for sentences with classical truth values and read '$\exists p(N(\bar{A}, p)$' as '$\bar{A}$ is the numeral of a sentence with a classical truth value.'

We can now introduce

$$\triangle(\bar{A}) =_{df} \exists p(N(\bar{A}, p) \ \& \ \triangle p),$$

in which '$\triangle$', as the real truth or knowledge predicate, applies only to the right type of sentences.

Paradox reappears. Analogues of our schemata will now hold intuitively for '$\triangle$', and there will be a sentence U such that

$$U \equiv \triangle(\overline{\sim U})$$

is demonstrable in the system. The argument will then go through as before. Note that if '$\sim U$' lacks a classical truth value, '$\triangle(\overline{\sim U})$' will simply be false.

22. It would be a mistake here, by the way, to think that by introducing '$E(\bar{A}, p)$' or the like we have somehow committed ourselves to an assumption that all sentences express propositions or that all propositions are expressible by sentences. No such general assumption is at stake. In the argument at issue, use of '$\triangle$' as defined commits us to claiming only that one proposition is known (or whatever) or is expressed by a sentence. An instance of schema (20) employed in the argument tells us that an instance of schema (19) expresses a proposition and that the proposition is known (or whatever). This clearly seems innocuous, and all other elements of the argument are hypothetical in the relevant respects.

23. It should also perhaps be noted that a stacked '$\triangle$' is buried in '$U \equiv \triangle(\overline{\sim U})$', since '$\triangle$' will appear in U itself. C. Anthony Anderson (1983, 350–351) gives reason to think that the deducibility relation $I(x, y)$ would have to be treated hierarchically as well.

24. In simplest terms, the basic distinction is the following. A predicate applies to a *name* in order to give us a sentence. A sentential operator applies to a *sentence* and gives us a further sentence.

25. See Ramsey 1927, 142–143. For Grover's work, see especially Grover, Camp, and Belnap 1975. Sarah Stebbins (1980) effectively treats redundancy theories as special cases of an operator approach.

Operator treatments of necessity are familiar from the work of Montague and Kripke, of course, and an operator treatment of epistemic notions appears in Hintikka 1967. An operator theory of belief developed with the general motivation of redundancy theories appears in Prior 1971, esp. pp. 19–20 and 131–143.

26. Heidelberger 1968. See also, however, Grover's comments in 1972. Further discussion appears in Haack 1978, 130–134.

27. One form of the derivation, using the principle that $\forall p \forall q (\S p = \S q \rightarrow . p \equiv q)$, is as follows. Given (29), if $\forall p (c = \S p . \rightarrow \sim p)$, then $\sim \forall p (c = \S p . \rightarrow \sim p)$. Thus $\sim \forall p (c = \S p . \rightarrow \sim p)$. If $\sim \forall p (c = \S p . \rightarrow \sim p)$, then $\exists p (c = \S p \& p)$. Let, for instance, $c = \S q \& q$. Then $\S q = \S \forall p (c = \S p . \rightarrow \sim p)$ and $\sim \forall p (c = \S p . \rightarrow \sim p)$, i.e., (28) and $\sim$(28). At a number of points here I follow closely Susan Haack's discussion in 1978, 149 ff.

Another form of the Liar using propositional quantification and some empirical assumptions, but without a truth predicate, can be formulated along lines suggested by Pollock (1971).

Consider S to be

$\exists p$(it has been asserted that p in the inner sanctum and $\sim p$),

where the inner sanctum is a special room in which only the Pope is allowed, and only when he speaks *ex cathedra*. I manage to sneak in, however, and assert that S, which is now true if and only if it is false.

Note also that the paradox would hold were nothing else ever asserted in the inner sanctum or, in a variation on the paradox, were nothing else asserted on certain lines of a certain page.

28. Here it would be a mistake, by the way, to think that by introducing '$\S$' or '$N(\bar{A}, p)$', we are somehow building in an assumption that all sentences p are nameable or "termable." No such general assumption is required. In the argument at issue, use of '$\triangle$' as defined commits

one to claiming only that one *p* is either known (or whatever) or termed: an instance of the second schema employed in the argument tells us that an instance of the first schema, for which there is a term, is known. This clearly seems innocuous, and all other elements of the argument are hypothetical in the relevant respects.

29. It might appear that one course for redundancy and operator theories here would be to explicitly prohibit term relations and term-forming operators such as '$N(\bar{A}, p)$' and '§'. In this regard it must be conceded that there are simple systems that do not have the resources to handle these, in which '$\triangle$' does appear as an operator with analogues of the schemata above, and which are provably consistent (here I am obliged to Evan W. Conyers for a group of particularly elegant syntactical proofs). It might be argued that in using propositional quantification and a term relation or term-forming operator we are, in spirit at least, violating Tarski's prohibition against quotation functions, legislated precisely with such truth-predicateless paradoxes in mind (Tarski 1935, 162).

There are, however, important limits to consistency results for operator systems: for sentential operators within some systems the diagonal lemma and paradox of the Knower will hold much as for predicates. I leave a technical presentation of such results to another context.

Effective prohibition of term relations, term-forming operators, and the like would at any rate have to be a recourse of heroic extremes. As Susan Haack notes in 1974b, quantificational forms of the Liar will arise with *any* means of denoting expressions, and we can expect much the same to hold for the Knower. A Tarskian treatment of quotation is, moreover, quite counterintuitive (see Anscombe 1957 and Haack 1974a), and quantification into quotational contexts seems both formally and informally to be of quite general and significant value (see especially Belnap and Grover 1973).

The case against a Tarskian strategy of prohibition is clinched, I think, by Donald Davidson 1979. As Davidson notes, any adequate theory of quotation—necessary for an adequate theory of truth—must do justice to the fact that "one can form the name of an arbitrary expression by enclosing it in quotation marks" (34–35). "If you want to refer to an expression, you may do it by putting quotation marks around a token of the expression you want to mention" (37). With substitutional quantification of the sort familiar in operator and redundancy theories, at least, this seems to be all that the argument demands.

In the end, I think, simple *prohibition* of quotation functions and the like would be comparable in extremity to simple *prohibition* of, say, a notion of truth, especially since, as noted below, a similar hierarchical treatment is adequate to hedge each against paradox.

30. Later in her work Grover takes a different tack. In 1975, 1977, 1981a, and 1981b she attempts to deal with paradox in terms of "inheritors" much on the patterns of Kripke's approach and the propositional approaches considered in section 5. As these affinities indicate, however, this later approach has nothing essentially to do with a prosententialist or redundancy theory. In the attempt to escape the Strengthened Liar, moreover, Grover seems forced to drastic measures, which even so may not prove effective: to insist that Liar-like sentences lack content, for example, but to prohibit concluding that they are not true (see esp. Grover 1977 and 1981b). In her later work, it might be noted, Grover also more or less concedes a role for 'true' as a predicate.

31. See esp. Burge 1979, 1981, and 1984. A similar account is employed in Anderson 1983.

32. Here Gupta objects that Burge's pragmatic rules "like all pragmatic rules ... are sloppily stated and do not constitute a theory of levels.... If we follow the Tarskian route then the theory of levels constitutes the heart of the theory of truth. It does not belong on the garbage dump of informal pragmatics" (1982, 28). This is not, however, the route that my criticism will take.

33. This is perhaps clearest in Burge 1981.

34. See, for example, Brody 1967 and Kirwan 1978, esp. 20–21.

35. One might attempt to avoid paradox here by insisting that the truth or falsity of (33) be represented by

$$\text{Tr}_{i+1}(\sim \text{Tr}_i(33))$$

and

$$\sim \text{Tr}_{i+1}(\sim \text{Tr}_i(33)),$$

which would block substitution of '(33)' for ' $\sim \text{Tr}_i(33)$'. One might even resist (33) itself on the grounds that formulas themselves, rather than their names, must follow 'Tr$_i$'.

This, however, would effectively be to propose that 'Tr$_{i+1}$' or 'Tr$_i$' be treated on the model of an operator, thereby both violating Burge's emphatic insistence that truth be treated as a predicate and introducing again all the difficulties outlined in section 5.

36. As a variation, consider the following:

Some instance of (ii) is not true.   (i)

$$\text{Tr}_i(\text{i})$$ (ii)

Are all instances of (ii) true or not? If every instance of (ii) *is* true, (i) is false. But if some instance of (ii) is false, it appears that (i) is simply true.

37. This might not even be theologically satisfactory, of course. It appears, for example, to conflict with a traditional notion of God's simplicity.

Chapter 3

1. I don't consider my purpose here to be that of a popular introduction to Gödel, however. That has been wonderfully done by others. See, for example, Nagel and Newman 1956, expanded as Nagel and Newman 1958, and Hofstadter 1979.

2. Which are the basic truths of a body of knowledge may, of course, be relative to the choice of transformation rules. Even given a particular set of transformation rules, moreover, there may be alternative sets of truths any of which might be taken as basic.

3. Judson Webb notes that "whether or not a discipline regarding a given subject matter can be deductively systematized is simply the question whether or not the set T of true sentences about that subject matter is recursively enumerable" (1968, 167). Of course, if requirements on "systems" are relaxed beyond recursive enumerability—as entertained in later sections—even this will not restrict those bodies of knowledge that might be captured as systems.

4. Just such an analogy between systems and (ideal) knowers forms the core of Smullyan 1987. There is also a significant amount of research regarding systems, knowledge, and knowers that has been done at IBM and SRI International but that is not yet widely known in philosophical circles. See, for example, Halpern 1986, Halpern and Vardi 1986, Halpern and Moses 1984, and Moore 1980.

5. It might be thought that the following is an additional obstacle to any comparison between knowers and systems: a standard formal system, if it is to exclude any formula as a nontheorem, must be consistent; knowers, on the other hand, are rarely if ever perfectly consistent.

As noted in section 7 of chapter one, systems have been developed in which inconsistency does not result in the inclusion of everything as a theorem (see, for example, da Costa 1974; Priest, Routley, and Norman 1989; and Rescher and Brandom 1979).

But at any rate, inconsistency cannot pose a problem here if we limit ourselves to formal systems analogous merely to *what a knower knows*. For no matter how inconsistent I as a knower may be in my beliefs, *what I know* must be consistent simply because what I *know* must all be true.

6. Hintikka 1967, 10. At a later point in the same work Hintikka proposes an alternative interpretation—that '*Kap*' be read not as '*a* knows that *p*' but as 'it follows from what *a* knows that *p*' (38).

7. Hintikka has since changed his tune, however. He now emphasizes that such a difficulty arises only if we insist that every epistemically possible world is also logically possble. See Hintikka 1975 and Taylor 1983.

8. We might attempt to model nonideal knowers and nonideal bodies of knowledge by using crippled transformation rules. In one way or another this is the basic strategy of a number of alternatives in the literature. See, for example, Eberle 1974; Moore 1980; Konolige 1984; Cresswell 1973; Rantala 1982; Rescher and Brandom 1979, chap. 19; Levesque 1984; and Fagin and Halpern 1985.

9. Strictly speaking, Gödel's own result was that any such system, if ω-consistent, will be incomplete. It is in Rosser's extension of Gödel's result that the stronger hypothesis of ω-consistency is replaced with the weaker hypothesis of mere consistency. See Rosser 1936.

10. The core of Gödel's incompleteness theorem can be seen as the diagonal lemma, outlined in the preceding chapter.

Because the axioms of G are recursively enumerable and its rules of inference operate only on finite sets of premises, the arithmetic relation $\Pr(d, t)$ between a Gödel number t for a particular formula and a number d encoding a derivation for that formula will be recursive. Because G is adequate for arithmetic, every recursive relation will be representable in G. There will then be a proof predicate $\mathrm{PR}(x, y)$ in the language of G such that for all $d, t, \vdash_G \mathrm{PR}(\bar{d}, \bar{t})$ just in case $\Pr(d, t)$, where $\bar{d}$ and $\bar{t}$ are numerals for d and t respectively.

Consider then the formula

$\sim \exists y (\mathrm{PR}(y, x))$

of G, which contains just the variable x free. By the diagonal lemma, there will be a sentence S of G such that

$\vdash_G S \equiv \sim \exists y (\mathrm{PR}(y, \bar{S}))$.

Syntactically put, within the bounds of consistency neither S nor $\sim S$ can appear as a theorem. Semantically put, though S cannot be a theorem, it will represent a number-theoretic truth.

11. At each step in such a progression we have, in fact, two options. To the axioms of system G we might add either S or, if willing to contemplate "supernatural" numbers and to reinterpret the quantifiers, its negation $\sim S$. We might then think of the pattern of "improved" systems in the neighhborhood of G as follows:

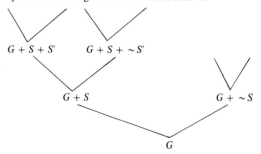

12. See Stern 1972, 511, and Church and Kleene 1936.

13. On essential incompleteness in this sense, see Tarski, Mostowski, and Robinson 1968 and Goodstein 1963.

14. See, for example, Benacerraf 1967.

15. For brevity, important details have, of course, been omitted. For a more complete treatment the reader is referred to the sources noted.

I have not included here work regarding systems with formulas of infinite lengths or nondenumerable alphabets. Leon Henkin (1961) originally considered three ways in which infinite formulas might be introduced: (1) by means of infinitary predicate symbols and hence infinitely long primitive formulas, (2) by means of infinitely long conjunctions and disjunctions together with quantification over infinitely many variables, and (3) by using infinitely alternating quantifiers of a particular type. It is the second of these that has been most thoroughly developed, in particular through the work of Carol R. Karp (see esp. 1964).

For some such predicate systems $L_{\alpha\beta}$, permitting conjunctions of fewer than α formulas and quantifications over fewer than β variables, completeness can be proven. A fairly uninteresting case here is $L_{\omega\omega}$, which is simply standard first-order predicate calculus without extension to infinite formulas. Jon Barwise, G. Kreisel, and Dana Scott have raised doubts about any such system with $\beta > \omega$, that is, admitting quantification over more than infinitely many variables (Barwise 1969, 227). But at any rate, where genuinely infinite formulas are at issue and a system's ability to handle quantification matches its ability to handle conjunction—where $\alpha = \beta = \gamma+$, for γ infinite—no definable system will be complete even if the underlying language has only one two-place predicate in addition to equality (see Karp 1964, 166–174). Nondenumerably many symbols appear in a system that Henkin uses to show completeness for first-order functional calculus (1949). See also Robinson 1965.

16. For details, see esp. Mendelson 1964, 258–271, and Wang 1964, 362–375.

17. See Mendelson 1964, 270; Wang 1964, 369–370; and Schwichtenberg 1978, 876–884.

18. A result attributed to Rosser in Wang 1964, 45, and in personal correspondence.

19. Feferman 1962. See also Feferman 1960 and Feferman and Spector 1962. Turing's 1938 work appears in Turing 1939.

20. As Feferman himself emphasizes, these results must be handled with care with regard to questions of completeness for transfinite sequences of theories. In general, the succession principle for a progression, such as (1), is not extensional—A_{k+1} is a function not merely of the set of axioms of A_k but also of some (arithmetized) description of the set of axioms of A_k, some intensional description. Because of this intensional character of the construction of recursive progressions, two transfinite sequences along different paths through the constructive ordinals O may have completely different sets of theorems, despite the fact that both start with the same initial system and satisfy the same basic succession principle. "Thus, questions of completeness of sequences derived from progressions hinge in part on more subtle questions as to how paths through O are obtained" (Feferman 1962, 262).

21. Trial and error processes at issue are still in a sense mechanical, however. See esp. Jeroslow 1975, 255.

22. The argument that follows is related to some wonderful work in Herzberger 1970 and 1981 and Herzberger and Herzberger 1981, to an incompleteness argument for finitary formal systems offered by Geoffrey Hunter (1971, 28–32), and to a Cantorian argument that propositions cannot be identified with sentences or classes of sentences offered by Hector-Neri Castañeda (1975, 34 ff.). A hint of the argument can even be found in Gödel's correspondence with Zermelo; see Grattan-Guinness 1979 (I am grateful to Gary Aylesworth for translation). The form of the argument offered here is perhaps most similar, however, to Johannes Baagoe's (1975). Baagoe's is a marvelous piece of work to which I owe a great debt.

23. For simplicity I concentrate here on merely one-place predicates and speak correspondingly throughout of properties of single objects. The basic argument would be the same, however, for all n-ary predicates and corresponding properties.

24. 'Capable of taking each predicate as an object' is not meant to obscure; it is intended merely to offer as general a description of relevant systems as possible. To fix ideas, one might think *fairly* broadly of systems that can be interpreted so that terms for objects can be taken to name predicates of the system. In full generality, however, the argument will also apply to "systems" that don't strictly have terms and in which the relationship between structural analogues of terms and predicates may not strictly be one of *naming*. In the end, all the argument requires is in fact that each predicate (or predicate analogue) of a system be assignable to a distinct object of the system.

25. As noted below, properties can be treated purely extensionally in the argument. Thus in place of 'all properties' here we might substitute 'all properties of membership in sets of objects'.

26. Throughout the argument, of course, 'How many?' is merely a matter of comparative cardinals. What is ultimately at issue is thus simply whether certain sets can or cannot be put into one-to-one correspondence.

27. "In fact," David Lewis notes, "the properties are as abundant as the sets themselves, because for any set whatever, there is the property of belonging to that set" (1986, 60). This is already true for properties extensionally construed; with an intensional construal in mind, we would have to say that the properties are at *least* as abundant as the sets themselves.

28. The proof, in brief, is as follows: Consider any set S and its power set $\mathscr{P}S$, the set of its subsets, and consider any function f that assigns a distinct element $f(s)$ of $\mathscr{P}S$ to each element s of set S. Consider further that set S^*, an element of $\mathscr{P}S$ consisting of all and only those elements of S that are not elements of their assigned sets $f(s)$.

To what element s of S could f assign S^* as $f(s)$? None. For suppose that S^* is $f(s')$ for some particular s' of S. Will s' be a member of its corresponding $f(s')$ or not? If s' is a member of $f(s')$, of course, it cannot be a member of S^*, since S^* is specified as including only those s's such that $s \notin f(s)$. S^* cannot then be $f(s')$. If s' is not a member of $f(s')$, on the other hand, it will be a member of S^*. And thus once again, S^* cannot be $f(s')$.

S^* cannot then be assigned as $f(s)$ to any element of S. Since f was taken to be any function mapping a distinct element of $\mathscr{P}S$ to each element of S, there can be no such function that doesn't leave out some element of $\mathscr{P}S$; the power set $\mathscr{P}S$ of any set must be larger than the set itself.

A form of the Cantorian proof phrased directly in terms of truths and sets of truths is discussed in chapter four.

29. In 1975 Hector-Neri Castañeda offers a Cantorian argument that propositions will outnumber, and thus cannot be identified with, sentences or classes of sentences. Castañeda also adds, however, "In spite of the preceding argument it may still be true that each proposition one can think, one can express—even if one expresses more propositions than one has sentences. This is an ontological justification of ambiguity. Perhaps propositions can be reduced to classes of sentences *and something else*, e.g., speech acts, behavior, and circumstances, capable of disambiguating sentences" (1975, 35). This last proposal, however, is clearly a mistake. Let me term 'disambiguators' whatever complexes of "speech acts, behavior, and circumstances" are included in the spirit of Castañeda's remarks. A Cantorian argument quite similar to Castañeda's original can now be constructed to show that propositions will still outnumber, and thus cannot be identified with, classes of ordered pairs of sentences and disambiguators. Contextual disambiguation cannot offer any escape from expressive incompleteness.

30. Here again it should perhaps be noted that the argument that follows is in a sense more philosophical than formal. The form of Gödel's incompleteness proof that it most closely

resembles, perhaps, is Gödel's own semantic and less formal presentation in the opening pages of 1931. Gödel himself notes a resemblance to Richard's paradox, itself but a step away from some of the Cantorian techniques employed here. A Cantorian generalization of Gödel also appears in Kreisel 1980. For further work on generalizations of Gödel, see esp. Wang 1955 and Smullyan 1985.

31. Here, as in the previous argument, as indicated in note 24, all that is ultimately required of self-reflectiveness is that each predicate be assignable to a distinct object of the system. I might thus have simply started with an f assumed to give us such an assignment, taking O_P as the set of objects $\{f(P_1), f(P_2), f(P_3), \ldots\}$.

32. Here and elsewhere in the argument, for noble motives of simplicity, I have unabashedly exploited a particular ambiguity. Though explicitly introduced as an object of the system, o_P is also allowed to appear as a term for such an object in referring, for example, to a formula $f(o_P)o_P$.

Somewhat more strictly, one might instead use $f(o_P)\overline{o_P}$ to indicate the formula at issue, where $\overline{o_P}$ is taken as a term of the system (a name or representation of some sort) for the object o_P. The argument can be rephrased with similar changes throughout.

33. Strictly speaking, this is a stronger assumption than mere consistency, but such a simplification is fairly standard in informal presentations of Gödel and seems harmless in the present context.

34. G. Kreisel notes with regard to a similar Cantorian generalization of Gödel that the argument can be applied "to situations which have very little in common with formal systems; to sets of axioms which are not recursively enumerated or 'listable,' to languages with infinitely long formulae or so-called infinitary rules, and the like" (1980, 172).

35. Here I use the power set without $\varnothing$, equal in cardinality to the power set itself, with the conclusion that there are more properties that are in fact instantiated than the being at issue knows to be instantiated.

Chapter 4

1. This was also, of course, the first apparent lesson of the Liar, with which we began in chapter one. In that regard the Cantorian argument that follows, which avoids many of the complications of the Liar and its replies, serves as something of a vindication of the initial Liar-like argument.

2. There is, of course, nothing special about t_1 here; any particular truth could be used in its place. There are also myriad other ways of constructing a truth for each element of $\mathscr{P}T$.

3. A more standard proof of Cantor's theorem appears in note 28 of chapter 3.

Alvin Plantinga, for one, is reported as saying that he remains "unconvinced" by appeal to Cantor's theorem. But such an attitude seems supportable only if Cantor's theorem is thought of as a purely mathematical result and any philosophical applications are thought of as merely metaphorical. The argument as outlined here, I think, makes it clear that this is not the case, that what is centrally at issue is a powerful piece of reasoning that can claim to be fully philosophical in its own right. It is by no means clear, for example, what step of the argument as outlined here Plantinga could try to deny with any plausibility.

4. Indeed, it is important that the truths at issue *not* be limited to truths expressible in some standardly finite language. At first glance it might appear that there is a conflict between the Cantorian result offered here and Lindenbaum's lemma, in terms of which we *can* construct maximal proof-theoretically consistent sets for familiar formal systems (see, for example, Hunter 1971, 110–111 and 177–178, and Mendelson 1964, 64–65 and 93). But the conflict is merely apparent, since (for one thing) Lindenbaum's lemma relies crucially on the fact that

wffs of such formal systems are explicitly finite. No such limitation is imposed on the truths of T in the argument above.

5. This is true at least in the ordinary sense of 'fact' in which it is a fact that $7 + 5 = 12$ and the ordinary sense of 'state of affairs' in which this is a necessary state of affairs. The notion of a set of all *contingent* truths is dealt with in the following section.

6. Does every conjunction of mathematical truths, even if it's a conjunction into the transfinite, correspond to a mathematical truth? If so, there is not even a set of all *mathematical* truths. Here the argument would be the same as the above except that for each element s of the power set, itself a set of mathematical truths, we would envisage a mathematical truth corresponding to the conjunction of all members of s.

7. Here 'truths regarding membership in sets of truths of type Θ' is only one possibility; much the same will also hold for sets of Θ truths and other relations. If all truths about one or more Θ truths themselves count as Θ truths, for example, it will again be impossible for there to be a set of all Θ truths.

8. I am indebted to Allen Hazen for suggesting this possibility in correspondence.

9. Sobel, in personal correspondence.

10. All of this is not, I am told, entirely without theological precedent: Aquinas claims that to each degree of being there corresponds a being.

11. See also Plantinga 1974a, 34–44, and 1974b, 44–69. As noted in chapter one, something very like Adams' and Plantinga's maximality approach to possible worlds seems to trace all the way back to Leibniz. See Brown 1987.

This is not, of course, the only way that possible worlds have been introduced. In Lewis 1973, for example, possible worlds are ways things might have been. In Slote 1975 they are possible histories of the world. In Stalnaker 1976 possible worlds are, as in Lewis, "ways things could have been," but Stalnaker envisages the "ways" as abstract objects in their own right. Though none of these alternatives is outlined in terms of a maximality condition as explicit as that in Plantinga and Adams, it might be argued that such a condition is implicitly required in these accounts as well.

12. Something like this form of the argument appears also in Bringsjord 1985.

13. Somewhat less central to present concerns is a Cantorian argument against a set of all worlds that appears in Davies 1981, 262, with credit to David Kaplan and Christopher Peacocke, and in several papers by Michael Jubien (1987a and 1987b). See also, however, David Lewis's response to such an argument in 1986, 104–108.

14. See, for example, Copi 1979, 179.

15. Here I have not included a separate treatment of Peter Aczel's ZFC/AFA (1987 and 1988), discussed in connection with Barwise and Etchemendy's *The Liar* (1987) in chapter one. Despite features of quite general interest, it turns out that ZFC/AFA doesn't add anything of major importance to the present discussion. In particular, as indicated in note 51 of chapter one, ZFC/AFA doesn't offer any new approach to Russellian or Cantorian difficulties. In Barwise and Etchemendy these are simply passed on to classes beyond ZFC/AFA proper, and thus basic questions are still left to one or another of the alternative class theories at issue in the text.

16. Specker's work is discussed in Quine 1969, 294–299.

17. This enlargement is not, Quine is careful to note, an *extension* in the technical sense of the term: axioms of NF must be relativized to sets in the transition to ML, rather than simply supplemented.

18. Quine 1969, 307–308. The axiom of choice still fails in the strong form 'Every set of exclusive sets has a selection set', but it apparently can be assumed for ML in the form 'Every set (or even every class) of exclusive sets has a selection *class*'.

Hao Wang charges, on the basis of a result attributed to Rosser, that if NF is consistent, the class Nn of natural numbers cannot be a set within ML (Wang 1986, 640). As Quine notes, however, the real Rosser result is significantly weaker: that if NF is consistent, within ML Nn cannot be *proven* to be a set (Quine 1986).

19. ML can have no Russellian *set* $\hat{u}(u \notin u)$, for the standard reasons (Quine 1969, 309). The possibility of sethood for $\hat{u}(u = u)$ is a trickier question. Whether $\bigcup V \in \bigcup V$ or is itself an ultimate class, Quine tells us, is a matter "we are free to settle by further postulation" (300). But sethood is even a prospect for $\bigcup V$ only because the crippling of Cantor's theorem in the form $z < \hat{u}(u \subseteq z)$ remains in effect as a leftover feature from NF.

20. The general Cantorian argument that any set will be smaller than its power set fails to go through in ML because of lack of assurance that sets satisfying any condition C (in particular, sets satisfying a "diagonalization" condition) will form a set. But here we *are* assured that the *truths* satisfying any condition C will form a set, and thus the Cantorian argument against a set of all *truths* will go through without a hitch.

21. Were such a system seriously pursued, of course, we would probably also want classes containing both sets and truths. Were the variant of ML outlined above seriously pursued, we would also presumably want sets containing both sets and truths.

22. Here it is instructive to note the difference between a class of all sets, which can exist within ML-like systems, and a class of all truths, which cannot. A Cantorian argument against a class of all sets $\bigcup V$ is blocked because the "diagonalized" subclass of $\bigcup V$ crucial to the argument is not guaranteed to be a set and thus is not guaranteed to be a member too many of $\bigcup V$. Against a class of all *truths*, however, the Cantorian argument does hold, because here we need merely a *truth* rather than a *set* for each subclass of the class in question.

23. A further option for an ML-like system, not attempted here, might be to admit only sets of truths, as in the first variation above, but to admit even these only subject to stratification requirements: only for stratified conditions C will there be a set of those truths satisfying C.

But even this would not suffice to save a set of all truths, for very much the same reasons as those detailed against ZF — power in section 4. Stratification requirements within ML are written in terms of restrictions on '∈'. But the Cantorian argument against a set of all truths need not be written in terms of sets and membership. As indicated in the following section, such an argument can be written instead simply in terms of truths *about* truths, and that form of the argument would be one that stratification restrictions on '∈' would be insufficient to block.

24. See Lévy 1976, 181.

25. This assumes that '≤' is defined standardly, in Quine's terms, as

'$y \leq z$' for '∃w(Func w & $y \subseteq w``z$)'.

If, on the other hand, we were to redefine '≤' as

'$y \leq z$' for '∃w(Func w & $w \in \bigcup V$ & $y \subseteq w``z$)',

we would be in the same position as in ML: Cantor's theorem in this form *would* be provable, and a class of all truths would face ML-like difficulties as before. See Quine 1963, 314.

26. Other forms of Cantorian argument against a class of all truths may not be so easily avoided. Consider, for example, not subclasses of T, as above, but merely *conditions*, conditions that may or may not define subclasses on elements of T. We will have the condition for C^*, for example, even if that condition fails to define a class. Now there will be more such conditions on elements of T than elements of T, and for each such condition there will be a truth—that it *is* a condition, for example, or that it does or does not define a class. On this form of the argument, then, it appears that there *still* could be no class of all truths.

27. Essentially the same system appears as Quine-Morse (QM) in Lévy 1976, and as Bernays-Morse in Chang and Keisler 1973, 510–511. The strategy of widening the comprehension axiom of VNB to impredicative cases is also introduced in Quine 1963, 321.

28. For a discussion of difficulties and alternatives in interpreting A, see Wang 1977.

29. This does not, of course, hold in reverse: class statements of A have no natural representation within ZF.

30. In general, of course, it can also be argued that alternative set theories demand a cluttered and less natural choice of primitive notions. Indeed, it's far from clear what intuitively distinguishes classes from sets, or why we should think there is a second level of collections above and beyond collections offered by sets. See Kuratowski and Mostowski 1966, 57–58, and Grim and Mar 1989.

31. This doesn't *quite* hold for Ackerman set theory. Though comprehension for classes explicitly introduces only classes of sets, it is provable in A that there are classes not all of whose members are sets. Nonetheless, provision in A for such classes seems minimal, and Quine's lament still applies: "We want to be able to form finite classes, in all ways, of all things there are assumed to be …, and the trouble is that ultimate classes will not belong" (1969, 321).

32. VNB modified is a close relative of KM, as indicated in note 27.

33. Menzel 1986b. See also Bringsjord 1985 and Grim 1984, 1986, and 1990.

34. Menzel's reasons for rejecting VNB and the like are significantly different, however, from those offered in section 3 above.

In 1986a Menzel distinguishes two conditions on proper classes: excessive size (within VNB, proper classes are those too large to be sets) and unbounded rank (where the *rank* of an object is defined recursively as the least ordinal greater than the ranks of all its members, and a class is said to be *unbounded* if it contains members of arbitrarily high rank). It is the second of these that Menzel takes as the "true conceptual boundary" between sets and proper classes. If propositions (or truths) are admitted as ur-elements, however, a world story (or totality of truths) S will be of *bounded* rank: "Since … propositions for the world-story theorist are not sets, they themselves have no members and so have a rank of 0; hence, S itself has a rank of 1, i.e. S is bounded" (Menzel 1986a/b, 70). There is then no need to consign world stories (or a totality of truths) to the realm of proper classes. Or so the argument goes.

Note, however, that Menzel's "ranks" here are confined exclusively to sets: sets alone have ranks, determined exclusively by the ranks of their members. But this may be a dangerously provincial view of rank. Hierarchies of types have often been thought necessary for propositions, predicates, and properties as well as sets, and in the end an *integrated* theory of types may be required.

We may find it necessary to rank sets of propositions about those sets mentioned in propositions they include, for example, in order to deal with problems such as the following variant of Russell's paradox:

Some sets of propositions contain propositions that mention those sets themselves. Some sets of propositions contain no such propositions. Let us refer to the latter as non-self-mentioning propositional sets. Consider now the set S' of all propositions that mention only non-self-mentioning sets. Is S' self-mentioning or not?

Yet given an *integrated* ranking, one that includes propositions and perhaps predicates and properties as well as sets, Menzel's argument fails to go through. In particular, it is no longer clear that world stories will have a rank of 1 or any other bounded n.

On the other hand, as indicated in section 3, there *do* seem to be strong reasons to think that Menzel's *conclusion* here is right: that the proper or ultimate classes of VNB and similar systems cannot prove adequate for world stories or totalities of truths.

In a later piece, it should be added, Menzel does pay serious attention to "mixed" Russellian paradoxes, such as that offered above. See Menzel 1987. Regarding integrated hierarchies of sets, properties, and propositions, see also Fine 1977.

35. As a way of allowing for large sets, Menzel notes, "This could be done essentially as in [Menzel 1986a], viz. the large sets are defined to be just those sets which are not in one-to-one correspondence with any pure set, i.e. any set whose transitive closure contains only sets. Restriction of the axiom schema of replacement to 'small' sets is also necessary" (Menzel 1986b, 71).

36. Some surprising technical limitations of ZF − power appear in Zarach 1982.

37. Interestingly enough, a relative of the argument appears in Russell 1903 against a totality of propositions, phrased in terms of propositions of the form 'every m is true'.

38. Technically, of course, conditions $B(x)$ within pure ZF are formulas of first-order logic. Here what is at issue is a form of ZF − power and a form of the separation axiom based on a significantly richer language, a language appropriate, for example, for dealing with truths as well.

39. See, for example, Lévy 1976, 175.

40. Note that this is not a problem for sets in ZF − power in general: the argument above relies essentially on the supposition that T is a set of all *truths*.

41. One charge that can be leveled against such an account, of course, is circularity. See, for example, Fine 1985.

42. An outline for possible worlds that similarly uses entailment to avoid 'inclusion' or 'containment' appears in Menzel 1986b, 72.

43. The complications of this definition, as well as some neglected difficulties in defining omniscience in general, are discussed in note 7 of chapter one.

44. With an eye to the interpretation of second-order formulas, George Boolos has proposed a similar abandonment of formal semantics (see esp. 1984, 1985, and 1975). Consider, for example,

There are some sets such that no one of them is a member of itself and also such that every set that is not a member of itself is one of them,   (i)

or more simply

There are some sets that are all the non-self-membered sets.   (ii)

Each of these sentences, Boolos insists, expresses a simple truth. But if we represent them in second-order notation as

$$\exists X (\exists x X x \ \& \ \forall x (X x \equiv \ \sim x \in x),$$ (iii)

with individual variables ranging over sets, and if we go on to read '$\exists X$' standardly as 'there is a set X' and read '$X x$' as 'x is a member of X', what we end up with is the simple falsehood that there is a set of all non-self-membered sets. Boolos gives a slightly different example:

> There are certain sentences that cannot be analyzed as expressing statements about collections in the manner suggested, e.g., "There are some sets that are self-identical, and every set that is not a member of itself is one of them." That sentence says something trivially true; but the sentence "There is a collection of sets that are self-identical, and every set that is not a member of itself is a member of this collection," which is supposed to make its meaning explicit, says something false. (Boolos 1984, 446–447)

Boolos rejects the idea of merely substituting classes for sets in the interpretation of second-order formulas ("These constructions do not ... need to be understood as quantifying over any sort of 'big' objects which have members and which 'would be' sets 'but for' their size" [Boolos 1984, 447]), which would at any rate leave us with the same problem in terms of (iv):

There are some classes that are all the non-self-membered ones.   (iv)

What Boolos suggests in place of *any* formal semantics in terms of *any* sort of collection is that when asked for the interpretation of second-order formulas, we should fall back immediately on the *in*formal plural noun constructions of *natural* language.

How are we to interpret second-order formulas without appeal to the troublesome collections of a formal semantics?

> There is a simple answer. Abandon, if one ever had it, the idea that use of plural forms must always be understood to commit one to the existence of sets (or "classes" or "collections" or "totalities") of those things to which the corresponding singleton forms apply. The idea is untenable in general in any event: There are some sets of which every set that is not a member of itself is one, but there is no set of which every set that is not a member of itself is a member, as the reader, understanding English and knowing some set theory, is doubtless prepared to agree. Then, using the plural forms that are available in one's mother tongue, translate the formulas into that tongue and see that the resulting English (or whatever) sentences express true statements. The sentences that arise in this way will lack the trenchancy of memorable aphorisms, but they will be proper sentences of English which, with a modicum of difficulty, can be understood and seen to say something true. (Boolos 1984, 442)

The '$\exists X$' of second-order formulas such as (iii), then, is not on Boolos's account to be read in terms of any set, class, collection, or totality of any formal semantics whatsoever. Second-order variables in general are instead to be interpreted directly in terms of informal English plural noun phrases. If we read individual variables as ranging over sets, for example, (iii) simply amounts to (ii).

It does *not* appear, however, that such a proposal really offers any genuine escape from the Russellian problems that motivated it. The Russellian problems that Boolos attempts to avoid arise within a set-theoretic semantics when we quantify over sets and also arise within a class-theoretic semantics when we quantify over classes. His alternative, we've seen, is a direct appeal to the plural-noun constructions of natural language.

But we can resurrent precisely the same sort of Russellian problem, this time for Boolos's *in*formal semantics of plural noun phrases, by considering a language rich enough to quantify over plural noun phrases and to express some of their basic properties. Consider, for example, the following second-order formula:

$$\exists X(\exists x X x \; \& \; \forall x[X x \equiv \; \sim A x x]), \tag{v}$$

where 'x' is taken as ranging over plural noun phrases and '$\sim A x x$' is taken to indicate that a noun phrase does not apply to itself (in the familiar sense that 'dog' does apply to Rover, among other canines, but does not apply to Puss).

There seems no reason to think that (v) does not express a simple truth—the truth, for example, that there is a set X of which each non-self-applicable plural noun phrase is a member. If Boolos's proposal is to apply to second-order quantification in general, however, his informal semantics would force us to read (v) as (vi):

There are some plural noun phrases that are all the plural noun phrases
that do not apply to themselves.   (vi)

But this is simply Russell's paradox once again, here rewritten in terms of plural noun phrases and application rather than in terms of sets or classes and a notion of membership. For consider the plural noun phrase 'plural noun phrases that are all the plural noun phrases that do not apply to themselves' as it appears in (vi) above. Does *that* plural noun phrase apply to itself or not? Is *it* one such plural noun phrase or not? If it is, of course, it isn't. If it isn't, it must be.

At best, then, Boolos's appeal to an informal semantics in terms of plural noun phrases would merely replace a set-theoretic form of the basic Russellian difficulties with a plural noun phrase form of those same difficulties. But the fact that an appeal to natural language fails to solve the essential difficulties at issue should hardly be surprising. Russellian difficulties are notoriously familiar *within* natural language. To build natural language into one's semantics is simply to import them.

What the argument against Boolos above may more generally suggest is that there may in the end be *no* universally adequate form of formal (or for that matter informal) semantics. It is not merely that we need to replace set-theoretic semantics with X-theoretic semantics. For the type of problem that Boolos calls attention to with regard to set-theoretic semantics, quantification over sets, and a notion of membership seems bound to reappear for any X-theoretic semantics, quantification over X's, and some basic X property. Thus it may be that there is and can be no X such that an X-theoretic semantics would prove adequate in *all* cases.

45. I am obliged to Plantinga for this suggestion in personal correspondence.

46. A variation of the argument is possible in which we do without (1), but the form offered here is intuitively somewhat simpler.

47. There are, in fact, a series of major problems facing any such strategy. I leave exposition of more formal obstacles to another context.

48. Here too I am obliged to Alvin Plantinga for a suggestion in personal correspondence.

49. It should perhaps be noted that the force of this argument and others in the chapter is *not* against the notion of propositions per se. Certain difficulties for accounts of propositions in general were noted in chapter one. Here what is at issue, however, is whether there can be genuine quantification over *all* propositions—a question that would remain even if propositions themselves were entirely beyond reproach.

50. A strategy of "denying the diagonal" would seem no more promising here than before. To deny that there is any proposition that fits the form above would be to claim that it is an empty propositional form of some type. But there will then be more propositional forms, empty or otherwise, than there are propositions that P is about, and thus ultimately more propositions than P is about.

The target of the argument, it should perhaps be emphasized, is merely the notion of any genuine quantification over all propositions. That alone need not indicate that '$\forall p$' is without a use—that '$\forall p$' might not be used in all the standard ways as a quantifier relativized to some specifically limited domain of propositions, for example. The argument thus has significantly less to say about whether '$\forall p$' can be used formally in familiar ways than whether any such use can properly be interpreted as a genuine quantification over "all propositions."

51. There are also forms of the argument that don't rely on an initial appeal to identity but simply build the required function in terms of ordered pairs $\langle p, p \rangle$.

52. Here it might be tempting to attempt a three-valued treatment of 'about'. It's fairly clear, however, that any such attempt would fall victim to a strengthened form of the argument constructed on the lines of strengthened Liars and strengthened Knowers, considered in chapters one and two.

Chapter 5

1. An intriguingly different body of argument regarding essential indexicals, not included here, seems to add further support for the conclusion that omniscience must prove incoherent. See especially Grim 1985.

2. Rudy Rucker explicitly adopts a mystical position of this sort regarding a "set of all sets" V. See Rucker 1982, 196–218. It is not the case, however, that V simply fails to appear within any of a hierarchy of set theories increasing in scope. It is rather the case that within any set theory of the hierarchy the assumption that there is any V at all leads unquestionably and quite directly to contradiction.

References

Aczel, Peter. 1987. "Lecture Notes on Non-Well-Founded Sets." CSLI, Stanford, Calif.

Aczel, Peter. 1988. "Non-Well-Founded Sets." CSLI, Stanford, Calif.

Adams, Robert Merrihew. 1974. "Theories of Actuality." *Noûs* 17:211–231. Reprinted in Michael Loux 1979, 190–209. Page references are to the Loux volume.

Anderson, Alan Ross. 1978. "St. Paul's Epistle to Titus." In Martin 1978a, 1–11.

Anderson, C. Anthony. 1983. "The Paradox of the Knower." *Journal of Philosophy* 80:338–355.

Anscombe, G. E. M. 1957. "Analysis Puzzle 10." *Analysis* 17:49–52.

Baagoe, Johannes. 1975. "God, Ghosts, and Gödel." *Second Order* 4:32–35.

Bar-Hillel, Yehoshua. 1967. "Types, Theory of." In Paul Edwards, ed., *Encyclopedia of Philosophy*, vol. 4, 168–172. New York: Macmillan.

Barwise, Jon. 1969. "Infinitary Logic and Admissible Sets," *Journal of Symbolic Logic* 34:226–252.

Barwise, Jon, and John Etchemendy. 1987. *The Liar*. New York: Oxford Univ. Press.

Bealer, George. 1982. *Quality and Concept*. Oxford: Oxford Univ. Press.

Bealer, George, and Uwe Mönnich. 1989. "Property Theories." In D. Gabbay and F. Guenthner, eds., *Handbook of Philosophical Logic*, vol. 4, 133–251. Dordrecht: D. Reidel.

Belnap, Nuel D., Jr., and Dorothy L. Grover. 1973. "Quantifying In and Out of Quotes." In Hugues Leblanc, ed., *Truth, Syntax, and Modality*. 17–47. London: North-Holland.

Benacerraf, Paul. 1967. "God, the Devil, and Gödel." *Monist* 51:9–32.

Boolos, George. 1975. "On Second-Order Logic." *Journal of Philosophy* 72:509–527.

Boolos, George. 1979. *The Unprovability of Consistency*. Cambridge: Cambridge Univ. Press.

Boolos, George. 1984. "To Be Is to Be a Value of a Variable (Or to Be Some Values of Some Variables)." *Journal of Philosophy* 81:430–449. Reprinted in Patrick Grim, Christopher J. Martin, and Michael Simon, eds., *The Philosopher's Annual*, vol. 8, 1–20. Atascadero, Calif.: Ridgeview Press, 1986.

Boolos, George. 1985. "Nominalistic Platonism." *Philosophical Review* 94:327–344.

Boolos, George, and Richard C. Jeffrey. 1989. *Computability and Logic*, 3rd edition. Cambridge: Cambridge Univ. Press, 1989.

Bringsjord, Selmer. 1985. "Are There Set-Theoretical Possible Worlds?" *Analysis* 45:64.

Brody, Baruch. 1967. "Logical Terms, Glossary Of." In Paul Edwards, ed., *Encyclopedia of Philosophy*, vol. 5, 57–77. New York: Macmillan.

Brown, Gregory. 1987. "Compossibility, Harmony, and Perfection in Leibniz." *Philosophical Review* 96:173–203.

Burge, Tyler. 1979. "Semantical Paradox." *Journal of Philosophy* 76:169–198.

Burge, Tyler. 1981. "The Liar Paradox: Tangles and Chains." *Philosophical Studies* 41:353–366.

Burge, Tyler. 1984. "Epistemic Paradox." *Journal of Philosophy* 81:5–29.

Cantor, Georg. 1932. *Gesammelte Abhandlungen*. Ed. A. Fraenkel and E. Zermelo. Berlin: Springer-Verlag.

Castañeda, Hector-Neri. 1975. *Thinking and Doing*. Boston: D. Reidel.

Chang, C. C., and H. J. Keisler, eds. 1973. *Model Theory*. Amsterdam: North-Holland.

Chihara, Charles S. 1972. "Russell's Theory of Types." In D. F. Pears, ed., *Bertrand Russell: A Collection of Critical Essays*, 245–289. Garden City, N.Y.: Doubleday.

Chihara, Charles S. 1973. *Ontology and the Vicious-Circle Principle*. Ithaca: Cornell Univ. Press.

Church, Alonzo. 1976. "Comparison of Russell's Resolution to the Semantical Antinomies with That of Tarski." *Journal of Symbolic Logic* 41:747–760. Reprinted in Martin 1984, 289–306.

Church, Alonzo, and Stephen Kleene. 1936. "Formal Definitions in the Theory of Ordinal Numbers." *Fundamenta Mathematicae* 28:11–21.

Cocchiarella, Nino B. 1989. "Philosophical Perspectives on Formal Theories of Predication." In D. Gabbay and F. Guenthner, eds., *Handbook of Philosophical Logic*, vol. 4, 254–326. Dordrecht: D. Reidel.

Copi, Irving. 1971. *The Theory of Logical Types*. London: Routledge and Kegan Paul.

Copi, Irving. 1979. *Symbolic Logic*, 5th edition. New York: Macmillan.

Cresswell, M. J. 1973. *Logics and Languages*. London: Methuen and Co.

Da Costa, N. C. A. 1974. "On the Theory of Inconsistent Formal Systems." *Notre Dame Journal of Formal Logic* 15:497–510.

Dale, A. J. 1984. "The Illogic of Inconsistency." *Philosophical Studies* 46:417–425.

Davidson, Donald. 1979. "Quotation." *Theory and Decision* 11:27–40. Reprinted in Davidson, *Inquiries into Truth and Interpretation*, 79–92. Oxford: Oxford Univ. Press 1984.

Davies, Martin. 1981. *Meaning, Quantification, and Necessity*. Boston: Routledge and Kegan Paul.

Des Rivières, Jim, and Hector J. Levesque. 1986. "The Consistency of Syntactical Treatments of Knowledge." In Joseph Y. Halpern, ed., *Theoretical Aspects of Reasoning about Knowledge*. Los Altos, Calif.: Morgan Kaufmann.

Eberle, R. A. 1974. "A Logic of Believing, Knowing, and Inferring." *Synthese* 26:356–382.

Fagin, Ronald, and Joseph Y. Halpern. 1985. "Belief, Awareness, and Limited Reasoning." *Proceedings of the Ninth International Joint Conference on Artificial Intelligence*, 491–501.

Feferman, Solomon. 1960. "Arithmetization of Metamathematics in a General Setting." *Fundamenta Mathematicae* 49:3–92.

Feferman, Solomon. 1962. "Transfinite Recursive Progressions of Axiomatic Theories." *Journal of Symbolic Logic* 27:259–316.

Feferman, Solomon, and C. Spector. 1962. "Incompleteness along Paths in Progressions of Theories." *Journal of Symbolic Logic* 27:383–390.

Fine, Kit. 1977. "Properties, Propositions, and Sets." *Journal of Philosophical Logic* 6:135–191.

Fine, Kit. 1985. "Plantinga on the Reduction of Possibilist Discourse." In James E. Tomberlin and Peter van Inwagen, eds., *Alvin Plantinga*, 145–186. Boston: D. Reidel.

Fraenkel, Abraham A., Yehoshua Bar-Hillel, and Azriel Lévy. 1973. *Foundations of Set Theory*, 2nd rev. ed. Amsterdam: North-Holland.

Garver, Newton. 1978. "The Range of Truth and Falsehood." In Martin 1978a, 121–126.

Geach, Peter. 1977. *Providence and Evil*. New York: Cambridge Univ. Press.

Gödel, Kurt. 1931. "On Formally Undecidable Propositions of *Principia Mathematica* and Related Systems, I." Reprinted in van Heijenoort 1967, 596–616.

Goodstein, R. L. 1963. "The Significance of Incompleteness Theorems." *British Journal for the Philosophy of Science* 14:108–220.

Grattan-Guinness, I. 1979. "In Memorium Kurt Gödel: His 1931 Correspondence with Zermelo on His Incompletability Theorem." *Historia Mathematica* 6:294–304.

Grim, Patrick. 1979. "Plantinga's God and Other Monstrosities." *Religious Studies* 15:91–97.

Grim, Patrick. 1982. "In Behalf of 'In Behalf of the Fool'." *International Journal for Philosophy of Religion* 42:33–42.

Grim, Patrick. 1983. "Some Neglected Problems of Omniscience." *American Philosopical Quarterly* 20:265–277.

Grim, Patrick. 1984. "There Is No Set of All Truths." *Analysis* 44:206–208.

Grim, Patrick. 1985. "Against Omniscience: The Case from Essential Indexicals." *Noûs* 19:151–180.

Grim, Patrick. 1986. "On Sets and Worlds: A Reply to Menzel." *Analysis* 46:186–191.

Grim, Patrick. 1988. "Logic and Limits of Knowledge and Truth." *Noûs* 22:341–367.

Grim, Patrick. 1990. "On Omniscience and a 'Set of All Truths': A Reply to Bringsjord." *Analysis* 50:271–276.

Grim, Patrick, and Gary Mar. 1989. "On Situations and the World." *Analysis* 49:143–148.

Grover, Dorothy L. 1968. "The Indispensability of Truth." *American Philosophical Quarterly* 5:212–217.

Grover, Dorothy L. 1972. "Propositional Quantifiers." *Journal of Philosophical Logic* 1:111–136.

Grover, Dorothy L. 1973. "Propositional Quantification and Quotation Contexts." In Hugues Leblanc, ed., *Truth, Syntax, and Modality*, 17–47. London: North-Holland.

Grover, Dorothy L. 1975. "'This Is False' on the Prosententialist Theory." *Analysis* 36:80–83.

Grover, Dorothy L. 1977. "Inheritors and Paradox." *Journal of Philosophy* 74:590–604.

Grover, Dorothy L. 1981a. "Truth." *Philosophia* 10:225–252.

Grover, Dorothy L. 1981b. "Truth: Do We Need It?" *Philosophical Studies* 40:69–103.

Grover, Dorothy L., Joseph L. Camp, Jr., and Nuel D. Belnap, Jr. 1975. "A Prosentential Theory of Truth." *Philosophical Studies* 27:73–125.

Gupta, Anil. 1982. "Truth and Paradox." *Journal of Philosophical Logic* 11:1–60. Reprinted in Martin 1984, 174–235.

Haack, Susan. 1974a. *Deviant Logic*. New York: Cambridge Univ. Press.

Haack, Susan. 1974b. "Mentioning Expressions." *Logique et Analyse* 17:277–294.

Haack, Susan. 1978. *Philosophy of Logics*. New York: Cambridge Univ. Press.

Hajek, Peter. 1977. "Experimental Logics and Π_3^0 Theories." *Journal of Symbolic Logic* 42:515–522.

Halpern, Joseph. 1986. "Reasoning about Knowledge: An Overview." In Joseph Halpern, ed., *Theoretical Aspects of Reasoning about Knowledge*. Los Altos, Calif.: Morgan Kaufmann.

Halpern, Joseph, and Yoram Moses. 1984. "Knowledge and Common Knowledge in a Distributed Environment." IBM research report RJ4421 (47909), IBM, San Jose.

Halpern, Joseph, and Moshe Y. Vardi. 1986. "What Can Machines Know? On the Properties of Knowledge in Distributed Systems." *Proceedings of the American Association of Artificial Intelligence*, 328–334.

Harman, Gilbert. 1971. "Substitutional Quantification and Quotation." *Noûs* 5:213–214.

Hellman, Geoffrey. 1981. "How to Gödel a Frege-Russell: Gödel's Incompleteness Theorems and Logicism." *Noûs* 15:451–468.

Henkin, Leon. 1949. "The Completeness of First-Order Functional Calculus." *Journal of Symbolic Logic* 14:159–166.

Henkin, Leon. 1961. "Some Remarks on Infinitely Long Formulas." In International Mathematical Union and Mathematical Institute of the Polish Academy of Sciences, ed., *Infinitistic Methods*, 167–183. New York: Pergamon Press.

Herzberger, Hans. 1970. "Paradoxes of Grounding in Semantics." *Journal of Philosophy* 67:145–169.

Herzberger, Hans. 1981. "New Paradoxes for Old." *Proceedings of the Aristotelian Society* 81:109–123.

Herzberger, Hans. 1982. "Notes on Naive Semantics." *Journal of Philosophical Logic* 11:61–102. Reprinted in Martin 1984, 133–174.

Herzberger, Hans, and Radhika Herzberger. 1981. "Bhartrhari's Paradox." *Journal of Indian Philosophy* 9:1–17.

Hintikka, Jaakko. 1967. *Knowledge and Belief.* Ithaca: Cornell Univ. Press.

Hintikka, Jaakko. 1975. "Impossible Possible Worlds Vindicated." *Journal of Philosophical Logic* 4:478–484.

Hofstadter, Douglas. 1979. *Gödel, Escher, Bach.* New York: Vintage Books.

Hunter, Geoffrey. 1971. *Metalogic.* Berkeley: Univ. of California Press.

Jeroslow, R. G. 1975. "Experimental Logics and Δ_2^0-Theories." *Journal of Philosophical Logic* 4:253–267.

Johnstone, Albert A. 1981. "Self-Reference, the Double Life, and Gödel." *Logique et Analyse* 24:35–47.

Jubien, Michael. 1987a. "Nominalism and Modality." Presented at Rochester University, May 1987.

Jubien, Michael. 1987b. "Models of Property Theory." Presented at the American Philosophical Association Pacific meetings, March 1987.

Kaplan, David, and Richard Montague. 1960. "A Paradox Regained." *Notre Dame Journal of Formal Logic* 1:79–90. Reprinted in Richmond H. Thomason, ed., *Formal Philosophy*, 271–285. New Haven: Yale Univ. Press, 1974.

Karp, Carol R. 1964. *Languages with Expressions of Infinite Length.* Amsterdam: North-Holland.

Kirwan, Christopher. 1978. *Logic and Argument.* New York: New York Univ. Press.

Kneale, William, and Mary Kneale. 1962. *The Development of Logic.* Oxford: Oxford Univ. Press.

Konolige, K. 1984. "Belief and Incompleteness." SRI artifical intelligence note 319, SRI International, Menlo Park.

Kreisel, G. 1980. "Kurt Gödel." *Biographical Memoirs of Fellows of the Royal Society* 26:149–224.

Kripke, Saul. 1975. "Outline of a Theory of Truth." *Journal of Philosophy* 72:690–715.

Kuratowski, K., and A. Mostowski. 1966. *Set Theory.* Amsterdam: North-Holland; Warsaw: PWN.

Kvanvig, Jonathan. 1986. *The Possibility of an All-Knowing God.* New York: St. Martin's Press.

Levesque, H. J. 1984. "A Logic of Implicit and Explicit Belief." *Proceedings of the National Conference on Artificial Intelligence*, 198–202.

Lévy, Azriel. 1976. "The Role of Classes in Set Theory." In Gert H. Müller, ed., *Sets and Classes*, 173–215. Amsterdam: North-Holland.

Lewis, David. 1973. *Counterfactuals.* Cambridge, Mass.: Harvard Univ. Press.

Lewis, David. 1986. *On the Plurality of Worlds.* Oxford: Basil Blackwell.

Loux, Michael, ed. 1979. *The Possible and the Actual.* Ithaca: Cornell Univ. Press.

Loux, Michael. 1986. "Toward an Aristotelian Theory of Abstract Objects." *Midwest Studies in Philosophy*, vol. 11, 495–512.

Mann, William E. 1975. "The Divine Attributes." *American Philosophical Quarterly* 12:151–159.

Martin, Robert L., ed. 1978a. *The Paradox of the Liar.* Atascadero, Calif.: Ridgeview Press.

Martin, Robert L. 1978b. "Reply to Donnellan and Garver." In Martin 1978a, 127–134.

Martin, Robert L., ed. 1984. *Recent Essays on Truth and the Liar Paradox.* Oxford: Oxford Univ. Press.

Martin, Robert L., and Peter W. Woodruff. 1975. "On Representing 'True-in-*L*' in *L*." *Philosophia* 5:213–217. Reprinted in Martin 1984, 47–51.

Maypole, Robert M. 1975. "Paradoxes and Many-Valued Set Theory." *Journal of Philosophical Logic* 4:269–291.

Mendelson, Elliot. 1964. *Introduction to Mathematical Logic.* Princeton: D. Van Nostrand.

Menzel, Christopher. 1986a. "On the Iterative Explanation of the Paradoxes." *Philosophical Studies* 49:37–62.

Menzel, Christopher. 1986b. "On Set Theoretic Possible Worlds." *Analysis* 46:68–72.

Menzel, Christopher. 1987. "Theism, Platonism, and the Metaphysics of Mathematics." *Faith and Philosophy* 4:365–379. Reprinted in Patrick Grim, Gary Mar, and Michael Simon, eds., *The Philosopher's Annual*, vol. 10, 91–112. Atascadero, Calif.: Ridgeview Press, 1989.

Meyer, Robert K., Richard Routley, and J. Michael Dunn. 1979. "Curry's Paradox." *Analysis* 39:124–128.

Millikan, Ruth Barrett. 1986. "Metaphysical Anti-realism?" *Mind* 95:417–431. Reprinted in Patricia Athay, Patrick Grim, and Michael A. Simon, eds., *The Philosopher's Annual*, vol. 9, 112–126. Atascadero, Calif.: Ridgeview Press.

Montague, Richard. 1963. "Syntactical Treatments of Modality, with Corollaries on Reflexion Principles and Finite Axiomatizability." *Acta Philosophical Fennica* 16:153–167. Reprinted in Richmond H. Thomason, ed., *Formal Philosophy*, 286–302. New Haven: Yale Univ. Press, 1974.

Moore, R. C. 1980. "Reasoning about Knowledge and Action." Technical note 191, Artificial Intelligence Center, SRI International, Menlo Park.

Moore, R. C., and G. Hendrix. 1979. "Computational Models of Beliefs and the Semantics of Belief Sentences." Technical note 187, SRI International, Menlo Park.

Mostowski, Andrzej. 1950. "Some Impredicative Definitions in the Axiomatic Set-Theory," *Fundamenta Mathematicae* 37:111–124.

Myhill, John. 1975. "Levels of Implication." In Alan Ross Anderson et al., eds., *The Logical Enterprise*. New Haven: Yale Univ. Press.

Nagel, Ernest, and James R. Newman. 1956. "Gödel's Proof." *Scientific American* 194, no. 6 (June): 71–86. Reprinted in Irving M. Copi and James M. Gould, eds., *Contemporary Philosophical Logic*, 14–34. New York: St. Martin's Press, 1978.

Nagel, Ernest, and James R. Newman. 1958. *Gödel's Proof.* New York: New York Univ. Press.

Parsons, Charles. 1974. "Informal Axiomatization, Formalization, and the Concept of Truth." *Synthese* 27:27–47. Reprinted in Charles Parsons, *Mathematics in Philosophy: Selected Essays*, pp. 71–91. Ithaca: Cornell Univ. Press, 1983.

Peirce, Charles S. 1868. "Some Consequences of Four Incapacities." In Justus Buchler, ed., *Philosophical Writings of Peirce*, 228–250. New York: Dover, 1955.

Peirce, Charles S. 1878. "How to Make Our Ideas Clear." In Justus Buchler, ed., *Philosophical Writings of Peirce*, 23–41. New York: Dover, 1955.

Plantinga, Alvin. 1974a. *God, Freedom, and Evil.* New York: Harper and Row.

Plantinga, Alvin. 1974b. *The Nature of Necessity.* Oxford: Oxford Univ. Press.

Plantinga, Alvin. 1976. "Actualism and Possible Worlds." *Theoria* 42:139–160. Reprinted in Loux 1979, 253–273.

Pollock, John. 1971. "The Liar Strikes Back." *Journal of Philosophy* 74:604–606.

Pollock, John. 1984. *The Foundations of Philosophical Semantics.* Princeton: Princeton Univ. Press.

Post, John F. 1973. "Shades of the Liar." *Journal of Philosophical Logic* 2:370–385.

Post, John F. 1974. "Propositions, Possible Languages, and the Liar's Revenge." *British Journal for the Philosophy of Science* 25:223–234.

Post, John F. 1979. "Presupposition, Bivalence, and the Possible Liar." *Philosophia* 8:645–650.

Priest, Graham. 1979. "The Logic of Paradox." *Journal of Philosophical Logic* 8:219–241.

Priest, Graham. 1984. "Logic of Paradox Revisited." *Journal of Philosophical Logic* 13:153–179.

Priest, Graham. 1987. *In Contradiction.* Dordrecht: Martinus Nijhoff.

Priest, Graham, Richard Routley, and Jean Norman, eds. 1989. *Paraconsistent Logic: Essays on the Inconsistent.* Munich: Philosophia Verlag.

Prior, A. N. 1962. "The Formalities of Omniscience." *Philosophy* 37:114–129.

Prior, A. N., 1971. *Objects of Thought.* Ed. P. T. Geach and A. J. P. Kenny. Oxford: Oxford Univ. Press.

Putnam, Hilary. 1978. *Meaning and the Moral Sciences.* London: Routledge and Kegan Paul.

Quine, W. V. O. 1967. Introduction to Russell's "Mathematical Logic as Based on the Theory of Types." In van Heijenoort 1967, 150–152.

Quine, W. V. O. 1969. *Set Theory and Its Logic.* Cambridge, Mass.: Harvard Univ. Press.

Quine, W. V. O. 1986. "Reply to Hao Wang." In Lewis Edwin Hahn and Paul Arthur Schilpp, eds., *The Philosophy of W. V. Quine*, 643–648. La Salle, Ill. Open Court.

Ramsey, F. P. 1927. "Facts and Propositions." *Proceedings of the Aristotelian Society*, supplement 7, 142–143.

Rantala, V. 1982. "Impossible World Semantics and Logical Omniscience." *Acta Philosophical Fennica* 35:106–115.

Rescher, Nicholas. 1969. *Many-Valued Logic.* New York: McGraw-Hill.

Rescher, Nicholas. 1978. *Peirce's Philosophy of Science.* Notre Dame: Notre Dame Univ. Press.

Rescher, Nicholas, and Robert Brandom. 1979. *The Logic of Inconsistency.* Totowa, N.J.: Rowman and Littlefield.

Robinson, Abraham. 1965. *Introduction to Model Theory and to the Metamathematics of Algebra.* Amsterdam: North-Holland.

Rosser, Barkley. 1936. "Extensions of Some Theorems of Gödel and Church." *Journal of Symbolic Logic* 1:87–91.

Rosser, Barkley. 1937. "Gödel Theorems for Non-constructive Logics." *Journal of Symbolic Logic* 2:129–137.

Rosser, J. B., and Hao Wang. 1950. "Non-standard Models for Formal Logic." *Journal of Symbolic Logic* 15:113–129.

Routley, Richard. 1981. "Necessary Limits to Knowledge: Unknowable Truths." In E. Monshek et al., eds., *Essays in Scientific Philosophy*, 93–113. Bad Reichenbach.

Routley, Richard. 1982. *Exploring Meinong's Jungle and Beyond.* Atascadero, Calif.: Ridgeview Press.

Routley, Richard, Robert K. Meyer, Val Plumwood, and Ross T. Brady. 1982. *Relevant Logics and Their Rivals*, vol. 1. Atascadero, Calif.: Ridgeview Press.

Rucker, Rudy. 1982. *Infinity and the Mind.* Boston: Birkhauser.

Russell, Bertrand. 1903. *Principles of Mathematics.* New York: W. W. Norton.

Russell, Bertrand. 1908. "Mathematical Logic as Based on the Theory of Types." In van Heijenoort 1967, 150–182.

Schwichtenberg, Helmut. 1978. "Proof Theory: Some Applications of Cut-Elimination." In Jon Barwise, ed., *Handbook of Mathematical Logic*, 867–895. New York: North-Holland.

Skyrms, Brian. 1978a. "Notes on Quantification and Self-Reference." In Martin 1978a, 67–74.

Skyrms, Brian. 1978b. "An Immaculate Conception of Modality." *Journal of Philosophy* 75: 368–387.

Slote, Michael. 1975. *Metaphysics and Essence.* Oxford: Basil Blackwell.

Smullyan, Raymond. 1985. "Modality and Self-Reference." In Stewart Shapiro, ed., *Intensional Mathematics*, 191–211. New York: North-Holland.

Smullyan, Raymond. 1987. *Forever Undecided.* New York: Alfred A. Knopf.

Sorensen, Roy A. 1984. "Conditional Blindspots and the Knowledge Squeeze: A Solution to the Prediction Paradox." *Australasian Journal of Philosophy* 62: 126–135.

Sorensen, Roy A. 1988. *Blindspots.* New York: Oxford Univ. Press.

Specker, Ernest. 1953. "The Axiom of Choice in Quine's New Foundations for Mathematical Logic." *Proceedings of the National Academy of Sciences* 39:972–975.

Stalnaker, Robert C. 1976. "Possible Worlds," *Noûs* 10:65–75. Reprinted in Loux 1979, 225–234.

Stebbins, Sarah. 1980. "Necessity and Natural Language." *Philosophical Studies* 37:1–12.

Stern, S. W. P. 1972. *Mathematical Logic.* London: Cambridge Univ. Press.

Swinburne, Richard. 1977. *The Coherence of Theism.* Oxford: Oxford Univ. Press.

Tarski, Alfred. 1935. "The Concept of Truth in Formalized Languages." In John Corcoran, ed., J. H. Woodger, trans., *Logic, Semantics, Metamathematics*, 152–278. Indianapolis, Ind.: Hackett, 1983.

Tarski, Alfred, Andzej Mostowski, and Raphael M. Robinson. 1968. *Undecidable Theories.* Amsterdam: North-Holland.

Taylor, Kriste. 1983. "Worlds in Collision." *Philosophia* 13:289–297.

Thomason, Richmond. 1977. "Indirect Discourse Is Not Quotational." *Monist* 60:340–354.

Thomason, Richmond. 1980. "A Note on Syntactical Treatments of Modality," *Synthese* 44:391–395.

Tomberlin, James E., and Frank McGuinness. 1977. "God, Evil, and the Free Will Defense." *Religious Studies* 13, 455–475.

Turing, Alan M. 1939. "Systems of Logic Based on Ordinals." *Proceedings of the London Mathematical Society*, 2nd series, 45:161–228.

Turner, Ray. 1987. "A Theory of Properties." *Journal of Symbolic Logic* 52:455–472.

Van Heijenoort, Jean. 1967. *From Frege to Gödel: A Source Book in Mathematical Logic.* Cambridge, Mass.: Harvard Univ. Press.

Visser, Albert. 1989. "Semantics and the Liar Paradox." In D. Gabbay and F. Guenthner, eds., *Handbook of Philosophical Logic*, vol. 4, 617–706. Dordrecht: D. Reidel.

Wang, Hao. 1955. "Undecidable Sentences Generated by Semantic Paradoxes." *Journal of Symbolic Logic* 20:31–43.

Wang, Hao. 1964. *A Survey of Mathematical Logic.* Peking: Science Press; Amsterdam: North-Holland.

Wang, Hao. 1977. "Large Sets." In R. E. Butts and J. Hintikka, eds., *Logic, Foundations of Mathematics, and Computability Theory*, 309–333. Dordrecht: D. Reidel.

Wang, Hao. 1986. "Quine's Ideas in Historical Perspective." In Lewis Edwin Hahn and Paul Arthur Schilpp, eds., *The Philosophy of W. V. Quine*, 623–640. La Salle, Ill.: Open Court.

Webb, Judson. 1968. "Metamathematics and the Philosophy of Mind." *Philosophy of Science* 35:156–178.

Whitehead, Alfred North, and Bertrand Russell. 1910. *Principia Mathematica.* Cambridge: Cambridge Univ. Press.

Whitely, C. H. 1962. "Minds, Machines, and Gödel: A Reply to Mr. Lucas." *Philosophy* 37:61–62.

Wittgenstein, Ludwig. 1921. *Tractatus Logico-Philosophicus.* London: Routledge and Kegan Paul, 1961.

Zalta, Edward N. 1983. *Abstract Objects.* Dordrecht: D. Reidel.

Zarach, Andrzej. 1982. "Unions of ZF⁻-Models Which Are Themselves ZF⁻-Models." In D. Van Dalen, D. Lascar, and T. J. Smiley, eds., *Logic Colloquium '80*. Amsterdam: North-Holland.

Zinov'ev, A. A. 1963. *Philosophical Problems of Many-Valued Logic.* Dordrecht: D. Reidel.

Index